Hawley Smart

Hard Lines

Vol. 1

Hawley Smart

Hard Lines
Vol. 1

ISBN/EAN: 9783337346355

Printed in Europe, USA, Canada, Australia, Japan

Cover: Foto ©Thomas Meinert / pixelio.de

More available books at **www.hansebooks.com**

HARD LINES.

VOL. I.

A Novel.

BY

HAWLEY SMART,

AUTHOR OF

"BREEZIE LANGTON," "SOCIAL SINNERS," "THE GREAT TONTINE," "AT FAULT," ETC. ETC.

"Of all the barbarous middle ages, that
Which is most barbarous is the middle age
Of man; it is—I really scarce know what;
But when we hover between fool and sage,
And don't know justly what we would be at—
A period something like a printed page,
Black letter upon foolscap, while our hair
Grows grizzled, and we are not what we were."

"The greatest miracle of love is the reformation of a coquette."

IN THREE VOLUMES.—VOL. I.

LONDON: CHAPMAN AND HALL,
LIMITED.

1883.

Bungay:

CLAY AND TAYLOR, PRINTERS.

CONTENTS OF VOL. I.

CHAPTER VII.

CHAPTER VIII.

CHAPTER IX.

CHAPTER X.

CHAPTER XI.

HARD LINES.

CHAPTER I.

THE CID.

YORK! Most of us know the pleasant, dreamy old northern capital on the banks of the Ouse, with its quaint, narrow streets, lofty embattlements, massive gates, and grand old cathedral. Except London itself, there is not a town in England that can conjure up so many memories of the past. Stroll home from the Knavesmire in August, and muse over the famous equine battles that have been fought out over that deadly galloping course for a half-trained one; we remember the scene when the mighty Blair

Athol went down there before a commoner, and caused the hearts of his St. Leger backers to sink into their very boots. As we rise the Mount fancy carries us back a century, and we picture to ourselves the feeling of exultation with which the travellers from the metropolis must have viewed the pinnacles of the Minster, and realized that their three days' journey was safely sped, despite accident of flood and field or reckless assault of highwayman. As Micklegate Bar comes before us it is hard not to recall the terrible rout of Marston Moor, and the scene of slaughter and confusion which occurred at the great southern gate of the city, and as we pass beneath the massive archway the grim remembrance of the display of heads on its summit which so speedily followed shoots athwart our brain, and inspires a vindictive feeling that heads lately used to our detriment would be more satisfactory to view there than on their owners' shoulders.

Next to Lewis Carroll's 'Queen of Hearts,' I have always regarded Richard III. as the greatest of historical characters from that one famous speech so poetically reported—

"Off with his head, so much for Buckingham!"

Henry the Eighth was very fair in this way, and his Royal daughter, the last of the Tudors, had a very pretty knack of shortening men's stature in this wise also, but they lacked the cynical brevity and quick decision of the last scion of the House of York.

What a wonderful old town it is! I could muse over it for weeks, and should then leave with a most unhallowed desire to dig it all up and look at those two or three other cities that lie buried beneath it. One looks up at the snow-white walls and fancies the steel morions and halberds gleaming above the parapet, and then remembers grimly what a mess the devil's dust, as used by modern artillery, would make of them in these days. Rare times must those have been when York held command of the Great North Road, and kept watch and ward at Bootham Bar over the restless reivers of the border on the one side, and a vigilant eye on southern treason from Micklegate Bar on the other.

Some thirty years ago, if you had left the city by Fishergate, near the Cattle Market, and made your way towards the cavalry barracks, you would have found shortly after clearing the city walls that the suburb ceased. Scarcely a house occurred till you arrived at the celebrated Light Horseman, a roadside tavern about half way between the city and the barracks, much patronized by the military, and celebrated as the place at which Turpin's Black Bess died. I am quite aware that it is the fashion of this day to deny that famous ride altogether. I make answer that, in these times of unbelief, we must remain faithful to some of the old legends, and this I have seen with mine own eyes performed often—on the Surrey side. At the bend of the road, a little after you passed the Light Horseman, lay to your right an old-fashioned country house, its gables wreathed in ivy, and surrounded by three or four acres of ground prettily laid out in gardens and pleasaunce; the dwelling this of Julian Harperley, banker, who, head of a very profitable business in the city, bore the reputation of a strictly just and honourable man. He stood well with all classes. He was hospitable, reasonably free with his money, and especially accounted fair and liberal in all his dealings. If things had prospered with him there was no hint of sharp practice or of usurious interest ever breathed against his name. A moderate sportsman, as every Yorkshireman is bound to be, and a moderate *viveur*, as most men were in those days, Julian Harperley was the *beau ideal* of the prosperous country banker, popular in the city, and upon excellent terms with all the county magnates that resided within reasonable distance. Julian Harperley was a widower, and in his married life he had been sadly unfortunate. About twenty years previous to the commencement of his history a Mr. Aysgarth, one of his partners, had been thrown out of a dog-cart and killed upon the spot. Business required that he should have frequent interviews with the widow, and the forlorn condition of the sorrow-stricken woman filled Julian Harperley's soul with pity. She was young and she was pretty, and, as often happens, her mourning became her wonderfully. Niobe in sombre draperies, with Psyche, in the shape of a little girl of five years old, clinging to her skirts, is undeniably attractive, especially to men verging on middle age. Julian Harperley was smitten with the love fever, took heart of grace, proposed, was accepted, and married the winsome widow, with little Annie included. She made him an excellent wife, and this was, perhaps, the happiest time of his life; but, alas! ere little more than a year had sped she presented him with a son, whose birth cost her life. She confided her little girl to his care, whispered him a faint farewell, and was gone, leaving the stricken man to bear his burden as he best could.

Annie, who was six years old when her mother died, was speedily a great solace to him. He had always been fond of the child, and now the little motherless thing stole her way into his heart completely. Her first passionate burst of grief over, and she seemed not only to sympathize with him in their mutual loss, but to transfer the affection that she had borne for her mother to Julian Harperley. She would creep up to his side, and nestle her tiny hand into his, until he felt impelled to lift the little maiden on to his knee, and once she had gained that desired position she would be quiet as a mouse, never interfering with his perusal of book or paper, save by a mute caress. That as she grew up she should become more and more to him was only natural, and undoubtedly Julian Harperley was the more delighted of the twain when, her schooling finished, she was solemnly invested with the keys, and proclaimed mistress of "The Firs."

A tall, handsome brunette, with flashing blue eyes, and plenty of vitality, Miss Aysgarth had not lacked admirers during the six years she had ruled over "The Firs," but no one could as yet flatter himself that he had made any serious mark in her good graces. Favourites she had, of course; but when man's vanity, as it occasionally did, prompted one of these to believe that he was valued above his fellows, he had been gently but speedily made aware of his mistake. A shrewd, clever girl, apt to fathom people's characters pretty accurately, and to appraise them at their fair value, and yet as she sits there this pleasant autumn afternoon, it may be doubted whether in her thoughts she is not putting a higher price on one person than he exactly merits.

It is a very pleasant place, that flower-gemmed garden in these September days—glorious days of a fine Yorkshire autumn. If they get their warm weather later in the Ridings than we do down south, it stays with them longer, and they are often having a gorgeous time of it when we are grimly contemplating the commencement of winter. The soft, velvety turf was bordered by old-fashioned shrubberies, through which trimly-kept gravel walks meandered in the direction of the road. Annie Aysgarth is seated in a trim rustic summer-house, kept with such evident care as to betoken it a favourite place of resort. She is occupied in piecing together some gaily-coloured bits of silk, though with what design is not easy of understanding. The mystery of a lady's work is generally above masculine comprehension. A light step on one of the gravel-walks running down to the road causes her to raise her head, put her work on one side, and resume the book she had been reading

"Ah! Annie," exclaimed the new-comer, as he emerged from the shrubberies, "I thought I should very likely find you here."

"Then all I can say, Harry, is, you had no business to think anything of the kind," replied Miss Aysgarth, laughing. "You should know I ought to be at the Dowton's, six miles away, but I felt idle, and so, somehow, you see, never made a start of it."

"Your besetting sin, my dear, is this want of energy," rejoined the new-comer, with mock gravity. "Ever since I have devoted my energies to the service of my country there has been nobody to keep you up to the mark. Two or three years back, and I should have decided that you required pinching, and—yes," he added, slowly, "should probably have done it."

"Two or three years back," retorted

Miss Aysgarth, laughing, "you were an unbearable schoolboy, whose ears I never could box sufficiently hard in return for your impertinence; but now, sir, bear in mind, you are an officer of dragoons, and as a cornet of horse are expected—"

"To behave as sich; quite so, Annie; but let's stroll up to the house. I want to see the governor. Is he in?"

"Yes; and how's the regiment, Harry?" said Miss Aysgarth, rising, and collecting her properties.

"The regiment is getting on very well, though the Colonel showed a painful want of appreciation as regards my military knowledge yesterday morning. You see, Cis Calvert was away, so was my brother sub, consequently the command of the troop fell on me yesterday at our drill on the Knavesmire, and I certainly distinguished myself, while as for poor old Copplestone he must have given the recording angel a hard time, and nearly used up the ledger."

"But why don't you learn your drill?"

"So I have; but when on your first mistake the chief goes off like a broadside of thirty-two pounders, who is to recollect it all? I should like to see you manage your cross stitch with a she-martinet invoking blessings on your head, and wondering how such an incalculable idiot found his way into the world. Smart commanding officer of the old school, Copplestone must have learnt his drill with that famous army of Flanders, I fancy."

"What is it you want to see papa about?" asked Miss Aysgarth, as she passed her arm affectionately through her half-brother's.

"I want him to give me another horse," replied the boy, for in sooth, he was little more. A good-looking stripling of eighteen, Harry Harperley, to his great delight and glorification, had some six months before the commencement of this narrative been gazetted to a cornetcy in Her Majesty's

—th Lancers. He was just one of those devil-may-care young gentlemen whom the public schools turned out in shoals in those days. In these times I fancy the affectation of the *nil admirari* rather spoils these frank-hearted youngsters; but I am writing, as may be remembered, of what has been jestingly termed the pre-educational period, when a knowledge of the 'ologies' was by no means imperative.

"You see," continued Harry, "we are not allowed to hunt our first chargers, much less race them. My second's in the school. I must have a horse I can do as I like with. It seems so deuced slow not to enter a horse for the Regimental Cup, too. I should like to have a shy at that, though I don't suppose I should have much chance against either Cis Calvert or Crymes."

"Major Crymes is no great friend of yours, is he, Harry?" inquired Miss Aysgarth a little anxiously.

"No, sister mine. He's a fine horseman,

and a good fellow, no doubt, but somehow I don't take to him. He rather snubs us young ones, and, what's more, I don't think the seniors care much about him either."

"Well, I am glad to hear you are not intimate with Major Crymes. I can't tell you why. He is always pleasant and agreeable enough when he comes here, and, to tell the truth, Harry, talks better than most men I meet. But he is rather cynical, I fancy."

"Can't exactly say," responded the cornet curtly. "He is pretty good at everything all round, when he takes the trouble to try; but he rarely plays cards, billiards, or anything else; hunting is the one thing he goes in for, and if he gets anything like a start he's bad to beat to hounds, even Cis Calvert acknowledges. But here comes the father," and as he spoke Julian Harperley sauntered on his hack slowly up the drive.

"Well, Harry," he exclaimed, as he

shook hands with his son, "are you going to honour us with your company at dinner? No one but Annie and myself to-night. We shall feel proud at the mess being thrown over on our account."

"No, father, I'll not sail under false colours. I am come to dine, but I am come begging, to boot."

"Ah, well!" replied Julian Harperley, laughing, "keep the petition till after dinner. Men's purse-strings, like their tongues, loosen more readily when that meal has been satisfactorily accomplished. If your request be not out of all bounds, and the housekeeper has not failed in her duties, I dare say you'll go back to barracks happy."

As the three gathered round the fire after dinner, Mr. Harperley pushed the claret across to his son, and said, "Now, Harry, what is it?"

"Well, the fact is, I want you to buy me another horse. I have only one I can hunt, you know, and two will be little enough to begin the season with."

"I make no objection to that; I always intended to give you a third. There will, I am afraid, be some trouble in getting hold of what you want just now. There are a good many men wanting hunters at this season of the year always."

"Ah, but I happen to know of one. You know Mappin, the dealer, who has the farm just off the old North road? I was out at his place the other day with Cis Calvert to look at a horse called The Cid—a clipper, a dark iron grey, with black points. Such a fencer, for we had him out, and Cis schooled him a bit. As he said, he's good enough to win the Regimental Cup."

"But if we bid for this paragon we shall be interfering with Captain Calvert, surely."

"No, no, father; you know I wouldn't do that. Cis liked the horse, and admired him immensely; but he said he couldn't afford him. He bought an old screw for a trifle, and said he must see as much of the fun as he could with that on the off days."

"It strikes me, Master Harry, I shall perhaps find the same objection to this grey that Captain Calvert did; the price is beyond me. What is Mappin asking?"

"Two hundred," replied Harry, "but he is well worth it."

"It's a stiffish figure, but I'll ride out there to-morrow afternoon after I get away from the bank, and if I am as much impressed with the horse as you and Captain Calvert seem to have been, I'll see if Mappin and I can deal."

"Hurrah!" exclaimed Harry. "We'll have the Regimental Cup on the sideboard before Christmas," and it was in a very jubilant frame of mind that he wended his way back to barracks shortly afterwards.

"You have sent Harry to bed in the seventh heaven," said Miss Aysgarth, laughing, as she bade her father good night.

"I always meant to give the boy another horse, as I said before, but they're always a little difficult to pick up when you want them. However, he seems to have found one for himself, so that problem's solved. Good night, my dear."

The following afternoon saw Julian Harperley riding leisurely along the North road, on his way to Mr. Mappin's, the dealer. That gentleman received him cordially, for the banker was an old and valued customer. Few men are more keenly alive to the infinite superiority of a cheque at sight to a bill at three months than those connected with the horse trade. Mr. Harperley's draft was as good as bank-notes; no wonder that he stood high in Mr. Mappin's regard.

"Very glad, indeed, to see you, sir," said the dealer, as raising his hat he emerged from a small counting-house in the yard, and advanced to welcome his visitor. "Here, Sam! take this gentleman's horse. You'll come in and have a glass of sherry and a biscuit, Mr. Harperley, before having a look round. I don't suppose you want one, but you like to look at a good horse, I know. I've one or two just now I'd like you to see."

Mr. Mappin inhabited a comfortable farm-house at Askham, about four miles from York—a low, one-storied dwelling, with thatched, sharp-pointed gables and latticed windows; roomy and commodious within, and boasting floors and staircase of blackest oak. The parlour, too, was wainscoted with the same material, polished till the panels reflected the gleam of fire or candle almost like looking-glasses. Adjoining the house was a large yard, surrounded on three sides by stabling. On the fourth was a large paddock, in the midst of which leaping bars and other artificial fences had been set up, while around the margin of the field a miniature steeple-chase course had been laid out.

Mr. Mappin was a well-known character for many miles round York. A lithe, wiry man of medium height, always scrupulously neat and quiet in his attire and manner, you might never have suspected him of being a horse-dealer; but you would have felt intuitively that he was an enthusiastic lover of the horse, and would have felt not a whit surprised at hearing there was no neater seat nor lighter hand in the East or West Riding. He had acquired a very high reputation in his vocation; those who had dealings with him were wont to speak of him as one does of the leading magnates of the wine trade, "You paid very dear, but you could depend upon what you got." He bought of course horses of all kinds, but his dealings were principally in connection with high class animals, and if a man wanted to pick up a good hunter in a hurry, and was good to write a stiffish cheque for the same, the sporting community round the metropolis of the north would have said unanimously, "Go to Mappin." Another thing, too, that tended much to the horse-dealer's popularity was the pertinacity with which he adhered to his favourite maxim—"Have the best of its kind, or don't have it at all." His wines and cigars were thoroughly in accordance with this axiom, and when he modestly asked a customer to share "his bit of fish and mutton," the salmon was fresh from the Ouse, and the mutton was four-year-old Scotch. Mr. Mappin was catholic in his hospitality, but at the same time he had all a Yorkshireman's keen eye for the main chance, and would laughingly say if reference was made to his prodigality, "Pooh! man, we never deal in the North without 'the luck-penny,' and a dinner or two is no great discount. That the wine is the best I can buy is matter of calculation; bad liquor breeds bitterness and mistrust, and might cost me many a customer."

"Well, Mappin," said the banker, after

he had deliberately disposed of a glass of Amontillado, "I hear you have a nicish hunter on hand—an iron grey, with black points. I have heard so much of him that I thought I'd just ride round and take a look at him."

"Ah! it'd be Mr. Harry told you about him. Yes, 'tis a nice horse, but I have one would suit him quite as well for less money. That grey, Mr. Harperley, can carry fourteen stone to hounds, and Mr. Harry don't as yet want one within twenty-eight pounds of that. Were you thinking of buying for him, sir?"

"I am thinking no more at present," replied the banker laughing, "than that I should like to see this grey horse."

"Very good," replied Mr. Mappin. "Try one of these cigars. If you'll excuse me for one moment I'll just tell the lads to bring him and two others down to the paddock. See 'em on the grass, sir, and you see what they are, and what they can do. These are all clever, put 'em where you like."

A few minutes more, and Mr. Harperley and the dealer were leisurely strolling through the paddock.

"You can tell a horse very fairly here," observed Mr. Mappin; "if there is nothing very big the jumps are of all sorts, and one that will school freely here in cold blood will cover anything his rider has nerve to put him at when hounds are running. If he don't, the odds are it's the man's fault; but here come the nags."

Mr. Harperley was fain to admit that the three horses that walked slowly past them in Indian file were all of good class; there was quality and breeding about every one of them, but there could be little doubt that

"The pick of the basket, the show of the shop"

was that grand iron grey with black points. Standing sixteen hands, with plenty of substance, he looked a weight-carrier all over. With those loins and quarters an extra stone or so should make little difference to him, and with thighs let down like that he was bound to gallop. Mr. Harperley fell almost as much in love with the horse as his son, and as he walked up to him and patted his neck, and looked at the small lean head and mild steady eye, he determined if the grey could only jump, and the price was not outrageous, that the graceless cornet should have the wish of his heart, and become the proud possessor of The Cid. But the banker had bought many a horse of Mr. Mappin, and was conversant with the wiles of that eminent dealer, and he noticed that the head lad of the establishment, the one usually employed to show off a horse, was riding not The Cid but a brown.

"I see you have got Sam up on the brown; the grey was the horse, remember, I particularly wished to see."

"Yes, sir, but The Cid don't want any

showing off, and I wanted you to see that brown horse. He'd just suit Mr. Harry. Take him down over the hurdles, Sam, and bring him back over the water. Sweet, handy horse, Mr. Harperley, he'd carry a lady well."

In Sam's experienced hands the brown acquitted himself admirably, but the banker was totally unmoved by his performance.

"Let me see The Cid, I think you called him, Mappin. When a man gets a horse like that in his eye, it's useless to suppose he'll look at another."

"Excuse me, sir, but though he can jump like a bird, I don't like risking a valuable horse like that over bars, hurdles, or water. It isn't business."

"Not business!" rejoined the banker in astonishment. "Why, you don't suppose we buy horses without to some extent testing their capabilities. You never made such an objection before. However, we know each other. I will take your guarantee that he's a made hunter. Now, name his price."

"I'm very sorry, Mr. Harperley, more especially as you have taken such a fancy to the horse, but he's not for sale, sir. I parted with him this morning."

"The deuce you did! What, I'm too late, am I? I suppose Captain Calvert bought him?"

"No, he looked at him, but didn't take him. I sold him to Major Crymes."

CHAPTER II.

MRS. CHARRINGTON'S GARDEN-PARTY.

THERE was, perhaps, in the days of which I am writing, no more prominent lady mixing in the society of York and its vicinity than Mrs. Charrington. A slight mist hung over her antecedents, but she was reputed to have been the daughter of some Indian official; at all events, Charrington, a cadet, of a well-known county family, who had been despatched by his friends to shake the pagoda tree, while the golden pippins still hung fairly thick upon its branches, had acquired both his wife and his fortune in the East. He was reputed to have had the ruling of a large tract of country, and to have squeezed those committed to his charge in somewhat unorthodox fashion. However, nobody could speak very clearly upon that point; communication between our Eastern Empire and home at that time was tedious and uncertain, and it was possible to deal out a good deal of arbitrary legislation without anybody in England being a bit the wiser. This, at all events, was certain, that ten years ago Robert Charrington had come back to his native country with a liberal pension, a very comfortable private fortune, and a tall, good-looking wife, some score of years his junior.

Mrs. Charrington had passed as a beauty in India, and it was not likely that she would renounce such pretensions on making her *début* in Yorkshire. Very much the reverse. If not quite a beauty, she was at all events a fine woman, and still adhered pertinaciously to the sceptre she had claimed on her first arrival in the country.

She was fairly popular. She had plenty of energy and go, and though much addicted to flirtation, her *liaisons* were all of the most innocent description, and if sometimes evoking sarcastic remarks from her sisters, had never drawn forth the stern condemnation of the veteran brigade. Mrs. Charrington had, unfortunately, one weakness which had more than once brought her into hot water. That she did not speak the exact truth was nothing; very few of us do. It was not that she indulged in malicious representation; she never meant any harm, nor had she any design of making mischief, but she was naturally a talkative woman. She had picked up that habit of continually discussing her neighbour's affairs so easily acquired in an Indian cantonment or country town, and she had a natural talent for embroidering. Her too lively imagination impelled her always to embellish such little histories as she might have to recount, and such delicate enlargement of course at times puts a very different complexion on affairs, causing some perfectly innocent incident to assume sombre hues, and suggesting a very background of darkness.

Still, despite madam's treacherous tongue, and her husband's arbitrary manner, the Charringtons were fairly popular. They kept a good house, about five miles from the city, entertained liberally, and, while Mr. Charrington, a noted pig-sticker and shikaree in his Indian days, could be relied on to promote all matters of sport in the neighbourhood, his wife was equally to be depended on as regarded balls, picnics, archery, &c. Mrs. Charrington has taken advantage of the fine autumn weather to issue invitations for a garden-party and dance. In these days lawn tennis would probably have taken the place of dancing, as in a previous generation the madness of croquet would have been the main object of such a gathering, but in fifty-two such things were not, and really an you disported not in valse, schottische, or polka there was nothing but bowls or sheer undisguised flirtation left with which to while away the time.

Mrs. Charrington's invitations had been numerous. It was currently reported that all the neighbourhood would be there, and as we know only let that rumour get about, and it fulfils its own prophecy just as a whisper of difficulty about obtaining cards or tickets for anything leads to every description of machination to procure them.

A showy, handsome woman looks Mrs. Charrington, as she receives her guests; though inclining to *embonpoint*, she still retains a good, if well-developed figure; the delicate bloom of her complexion may have vanished, and her face is, perhaps, somewhat florid; but the artifices of the toilet, and a profusion of fair hair, soften the slight encroachments of time, and she may still assert herself as a beauty, albeit a somewhat full-blown one. The neighbourhood has gathered in force; there are most of the dignitaries of the cathedral, besides a strong muster of the minor clerical lights of the city, the country people within a radius of some miles, to say nothing of that mysterious, but inevitable cohort of strangers who are brought, as a rule, by those least entitled to claim the privilege. Byculla Grange had the reputation of being a pleasant house, and the hostess was famous, not only for knowing how such festivities should be conducted, but for possessing the subtle art of imparting go to anything of the kind she took in hand. At present she is radiant with smiles, for has she not been vouchsafed a glorious day for her party? and who that ever dabbled in out-of-door entertainment can fail to recall how animal spirits at such times are regulated by the barometer.

When Robert Charrington elected to settle in his native county he naturally cast about for a residence. To find such a home as met the requirements of himself and Mrs. Charrington, accustomed to the ample house room of India, proved difficult. He at last solved the question by the purchase of Topover Grange, a farm of some couple of hundred acres, and pulling down the old farm-house, proceeded to erect on his new acquisition a mansion in accordance with the somewhat Eastern tastes of himself and his wife. The new building might be somewhat irregular in elevation, as Mr. Charrington insisted on the designs being carried out more in accordance with his own views than those of his architect, but the interior was exceedingly comfortable, and it boasted what in those days was by no means common, a luxurious smoking-room. Dr. Dasent in his *Annals of an Eventful Life* has drawn a very amusing comparison between the early Christians and the early smokers, recalling the times when the latter sacrificed to the shrine of their nicotian goddess in saddle-rooms, in out-houses, or it might be late at night in deserted kitchens, even as the early Christians had worshipped in caverns, ruins, &c., and further carries on an analogy by pointing out what sumptuous temples are now dedicated to the followers of both the creed and the custom. But when Robert Charrington's new house was erected smoking was still pursued furtively, very few country houses boasted a smoking-room, and not even some London clubs. When the Charringtons inaugurated their new home by a series of dinners, offering beds as well to their more distant guests, Topover Grange was pronounced perfect, and an invitation thereto a thing by no means to be neglected. But there it was; that was the crinkle in the rose leaves, that was the spectre in the Elysian fields, the fatal flaw in the paradise. "Topover Grange!" as Mrs. Charrington said, "it made her feel like a farmer's wife. It was impossible," she declared, "to live in a place called Topover Grange." In vain did Robert Charrington curtly tell his better half not to make herself ridiculous, he might have known better than to provoke such a contest. If he had ruled several thousands of Hindoos in right royally despotic fashion, he might have remembered he had never been able to make the wife of his bosom obey. He might be arbitrary, but Mrs. Charrington was pertinacious. They did not often differ, but when they did it invariably ended in the lady obtaining her own way, and such was the case in this instance. Topover Grange, as a name, being doomed, it became necessary to rechristen it, and in memory of many pleasant days passed at the famous Bombay Club, Robert Charrington named his place Byculla Grange. I don't think to people generally the new nomenclature conveyed much meaning, nor did they as a rule deem it an improvement, but to Mrs. Charrington, with her Indian recollections, Byculla Grange conveyed the idea of much magnificence.

"I am delighted to see you, Annie," exclaimed Mrs. Charrington, as she shook hands with Miss Aysgarth. "I always pride myself upon collecting all the beauty of the country at my gatherings, you know, and in that simple muslin and straw hat you look as if you had stepped out of a Watteau picture. Yes, there's nothing like simplicity, my dear, as long as you can stand it; but, alas! the time comes when we must dress," and the speaker glanced down at her own rich toilette with palpable satisfaction. "How do you do, Mr. Harperley, and where is Harry?"

"Harry will be here very shortly. He is to come with some of his brother officers. You forget that he is a dragoon now."

"Ah, to be sure, it had slipped my memory. We must hardly expect him yet.

The Lancers are always so shamefully late."

"Let me, in my character of the advanced guard, apologize for them," said a tall, dark, good-looking man, who smilingly advanced to do reverence to his hostess; "there hasn't been witnessed, Mrs. Charrington, such hard riding since 'the good news was brought from Ghent' long since—

> 'I sprang to the stirrup and Joris and he;
> I galloped, Dirk galloped, we galloped all three.'

There's severe spurring to be seen between Byculla Grange and the barracks just now, believe me."

"Ever ready with an excuse, Major Crymes," retorted the lady, as she stretched forth her hand, "so ready, indeed, that had I dreamt you were within ear-shot I'd never have ventured the accusation."

"Hardly a fair charge that, Miss Aysgarth, is it?" replied the dragoon. "I made no excuse. I simply grovelled on my knees and begged pardon."

"There's very little of that about you," rejoined Mrs. Charrington, drily; "but now you are here you must do your duty. Take Miss Aysgarth, and get her some tea, please."

"With pleasure," replied Crymes. "One moment, Mrs. Charrington, first—" and he murmured something in such low tones that only the hostess could catch it.

"Yes," she replied, with a nod, delighted. "Only you must wait till I am ready. Come for me when you see me a little disengaged."

Major Crymes bowed, and offered his arm to Miss Aysgarth. There was no reason why he should drop his voice in speaking to Mrs. Charrington. He had only asked her to give him a dance, but this was a way Horace Crymes had, and more than one woman had found herself on confidential terms with the Major without in the least intending it. He was one of those men to whom love-making seems a necessity, and he had left 'sair een' behind him upon more than one occasion, when too-credulous maidens had believed those low-toned whispers meant so much more than the actual words conveyed, and that the cool man of the world by their side was swayed by a genuine passion instead of merely seeking amusement.

"Are you fond of hunting, Miss Aysgarth?" asked the Major, having duly provided the young lady with some tea. "We shall be very soon beginning now in earnest."

"I am fond of it in my way, but I don't ride to hounds, if that is what you mean. I enjoy all the fun of a meet as much as any girl in the county, but I don't tax my male friends to either pilot or take care of me afterwards. I generally join what my brother irreverently calls 'the trotting brigade' for a while, and when the hounds go right away, come home."

"You have, perhaps, strong opinions on

the subject, and don't think it right that ladies should ride."

"No, indeed, Major Crymes," laughed Miss Aysgarth merrily. "Fancy a Yorkshire girl seeing any harm in hunting! But though not surprised, I feel rather sorry just now that you are so devoted to it."

"I am very much flattered that you should take any interest in my pursuits," replied the dragoon; "but why, Miss Aysgarth, regret my weakness for fox-hunting?"

"Because it has led to your forestalling Harry, and buying a grey horse that he had set his heart upon."

"That, I am afraid, is more your brother's fault than mine. He saw it, as did Calvert and others, before myself; but I never heard any of them were in treaty for it. I possess one virtue, Miss Aysgarth, and it's not a very common one. I can make my mind up at once. It has long been a maxim of mine never to miss buying a good horse if I have the money, and half-an-hour after I first saw the grey I wrote a cheque for him. If I interfered with Harperley, I can only say I am sorry."

The Major spoke very prettily on the subject, but showed no signs of giving up his right to 'The Cid.' Indeed, it was hardly to be expected that he should, and yet Miss Aysgarth had mistily fancied that she might do her brother good service in this matter. She was a reasonable young woman in the main, but was accustomed to see men make such little sacrifices for her sake. She did not, moreover, quite see the thing in its true light. Had she wanted this horse for herself it was just possible the Major would have resigned in her favour, albeit, the yielding of anything he coveted to another was a weakness Horace Crymes was especially free from; but the idea of yielding his new purchase to the last-joined cornet because his sister happened to be good-looking would have been simply derided had it ever crossed the Major's brain. He admired Miss Aysgarth, and wished to stand well with her, but nothing further as yet. He said no more than the truth when he boasted he could make up his mind quickly; he could whenever the necessity arose, and, having done so, would carry his determination out with ruthless persistency.

"Have you settled yet when your regimental races are to be, Major Crymes?" asked the young lady after a short pause. "It is whispered about that you intend to finish up with a ball at the barracks, and in that you know we are all much interested."

"The precise day is not fixed, but early in December, we think, we shall have fewer on leave before Christmas than after. May I have the pleasure of this dance?"

"Our valse I think, Miss Aysgarth," interrupted a laughing voice. "I am desperately late I know, and don't deserve it, but I must throw myself on your infinite compassion, which, like the dew from heaven, &c. Please don't punish me."

The girl hesitated for a moment, then bowing to Crymes, she observed, "I am afraid I am engaged to Captain Calvert," and took the arm of the new-comer. An angry light gleamed momentarily in the Major's eyes, but was almost instantly succeeded by his habitual *insouciant* smile, as muttering something about being more fortunate on some future occasion, he turned away.

It is, I verily believe, in the trifles of life that we evoke the deadliest animosities. It is astonishing how some people will brood over an ill-timed jest at their expense, biding the time when they can retaliate for such pleasantry with all the patient vindictiveness of an Indian. We forgive veritable injuries, but we cannot get over the culprit not having answered our letter of upbraiding. He neglected to pen that soft word which, lie though we should have known it to be, would have turned away our wrath.

Unanswered letters, perhaps, plunge us into as much hot water as anything, and yet, when the lengthy report of a 'breach of promise' case meets our eyes, we become aware that there is evil in too much letter-writing. Similarly, in the ball-room, it is quite possible to lay the foundation of a very healthy hatred—hatred which in the duelling days was promptly eased by a little blood, or it may be life, letting. In these more polished times we cherish it, and give more or less vent to it, according to the strength and malignancy of our natures.

Major Crymes up to this time had no feeling for Calvert either one way or the other, but this little episode converted indifference into active dislike. He was much too practised a man of the world not to see that Calvert had taken advantage of being *au mieux* with Miss Aysgarth to improvise an engagement, and she had consented to his ruse. The Major had so far merely regarded the young lady as a pretty girl, and with no particular attention; in fact, he was at present carrying on a pretty vigorous flirtation with Mrs. Charrington, and but for being thus piqued might never have troubled his head about Miss Aysgarth. Horace Crymes was a man whom difficulties always stimulated—a man for whom grapes out of reach, or forbidden fruit, had special attractions, and the quiet way in which, to use his own phrase, 'he had been jockied out of that dance' put two ideas into his head, to wit, a determination to be quits with Cis Calvert in some fashion, and that it was possible, perhaps, to accomplish that through the medium of Miss Aysgarth.

"I hope you will pardon my impertinence," said Cis Calvert to his companion as they took their place amongst the valsers, "but I wanted to talk to you so much, that I risked being properly snubbed sooner than forego the chance."

"And found me," interposed the girl laughing, "so utterly taken aback by your audacity or mendacity—which ought I to call it?—that I had not the presence of mind to rebuke it as it deserved."

"It was very good of you," replied Cis, "and your conscience may rest quite easy. I don't think Crymes had any idea that I was not really engaged to you. Let's have another turn."

"There you mistake," rejoined Miss Aysgarth, as she yielded to his encircling arm. "I don't fancy Major Crymes was in the least blinded by your bold assertion, and shall expect to find myself in his bad books for the future."

"A matter which will not concern you much," said Calvert.

"Who knows?" replied his partner, smiling. "He might get me struck off Mrs. Charrington's visiting-list. His influence here is supposed to be paramount, you know. Stop, there is Harry, and I want to speak to him for a moment."

"What? to comfort him for his loss?"

rejoined Calvert, smiling. "It is rather rough on the boy, but to hear him make moan over it is too absurd. If he had bought the horse and found it dead in the stable next morning, he couldn't be sorrier for himself."

"But, Captain Calvert, that is just what it represents to Harry. Papa would have bought the grey for him, and but for the unlucky intervention of Major Crymes the horse would have been now in Harry's stables."

"And it is a nag to sorrow after, Miss Aysgarth. I could have shed tears myself when I saw it, and found I couldn't pay for it ; then," continued Cis, with mock solemnity, "I reflected in my wisdom what a mildewed existence mine would become if I cried because I couldn't pay people, and what a vale of tears the British cavalry generally would be involved in ; but, come, let us go and comfort the bereaved one."

"How dare you laugh at me ?" cried the

young lady, smiling; "but take me across to Harry."

"Surely, Mrs. Charrington, you must have at last finished playing hostess," murmured the Major into that buxom lady's ear, "and have leisure to grant the dance you promised me?"

"Willingly. I am quite tired of making pretty speeches. I hunger to speak ill of my neighbours. Let us bury ourselves in the crowd, where I may give free vent to malice and bitterness. Ah! yes, I will valse, and you shall tell me all the gossip of the country."

"Ah, story, like the knife-grinder, I have none to tell; but that does not hinder our dancing—indeed, when one's tongue fails it is good policy to fall back on one's legs on these occasions. You paired me off unluckily, to start with."

"Unluckily! Why I sent you off with the banker's daughter, one of the best-looking girls in our parts, and this is your gratitude. I am a good-natured woman, Major Crymes, and, like certain royal ladies one has read of, always endeavour to provide for my admirers. If ever I did my duty for an adorer it was to you on this occasion. I paired you off with Julian Harperley's heiress, what more could you ask? It was a piece of self-sacrifice that should have ever remained embalmed in your memory, if a man ever does recognize self-sacrifice on the part of a woman."

"You are making too much of it. I only said unluckily, because the young lady and myself were not exactly in accord; besides, I don't appreciate being provided for. I prefer serving on your staff as yet. The royal ladies you quote so glibly, remember, only provided for an admirer when they had satisfactorily replaced him."

"True," responded Mrs. Charrington, with a coquettish glance, "and that is very far from my meaning, but you soldiers come and go, and it would be better to settle you amongst us than lose you altogether."

There was no great danger to the pair in this sort of flirtation. Mrs. Charrington had been engaged in these airy love triflings since her school-girl days, and, despite proverbs anent playing with fire and pitchers going too often to the well, had not scorched her wings as yet; love triflings that consisted of

"A little glow, a little shiver."

Horace Crymes on his side had passed a life of intrigue and flirtation. No woman's smile had quickened his pulse for many a day, but he still, from sheer habit, let him be where he would, was invariably engaged in a love-affair of some kind. There are men to whom such philandering seems a necessity, as essential to their comfort as tobacco, and having a similar soothing influence on their feelings.

"It is very good of you, but I had no

idea Miss Aysgarth was looked upon as an heiress."

"Of course she is. She inherits all her mother's property, to say nothing of what Julian Harperley may choose to leave her. He is a wealthy man, and has only the two of them to take care of. Annie Aysgarth will come to her husband with her hands full."

This was a fair specimen of Mrs. Charrington's embroidery. Julian Harperley's brief married life had been long a thing of the past when she made her appearance in Yorkshire. She knew nothing of the late Mrs. Aysgarth's affairs, but chose to assume she had brought her second husband a fortune. Mrs. Charrington, as a rule, invented biography for her acquaintances sooner than confess ignorance of their antecedents, which, as may be supposed, led at times to some asperity and confusion; but a taste for gossip or the *cacoethes scribendi* are no more to be grappled with than a passion for alcoholic drinks.

CHAPTER III.

SMOKE WREATHS.

Horace Crymes could hardly be pronounced a popular man in his regiment, and yet beyond a cynicism, by no means offensively obtrusive, there was nothing to be alleged against him. He was known to be devoted to the Turf, and believed by his brother officers to be a heavy speculator, but there was not a man in the corps who talked so little about racing as the Major. While beardless cornets discussed the respective chances of the Derby cracks, pronouncing judgment thereon with a confidence proportionate to their ignorance, Horace Crymes usually sat silent, as if the subject had no interest for him. The most direct appeal had never extorted more from him than he had been told such a horse would run well, and on the rare occasions he had so far abandoned his habitual reticence there had been found good reason for what he had said. He was, as Charley Harperley told his sister, one of those men who are 'good all round,' and it was whispered played very high when in London, but he never showed the slightest indication of a taste for gambling amongst his comrades. He seldom touched a card, and when to make up a rubber he sat down to whist, seemed perfectly contented with the usual regimental points. It was known, too, that he had three or four horses in training, but with these he pursued the same policy, never entering them in any races got up by the corps, or even by the garrison in which he might be quartered, but leaving them to pursue their chequered career on country race-courses, where in

Tally-Ho stakes and Goneaway Plates they were all more or less known. The Major had, however, one peculiarity quite sufficient to account for his not being exactly popular with his brother officers—he lived his own life. He would contribute handsomely to anything they might wish to get up, such as balls or other festivals; he was courteous and on good terms with them all, but he was intimate with none. He went] his own way, and was rarely seen either walking or riding with his comrades. He was a man, moreover, about whom little was known; no one in the regiment could tell anything about his friends, nor even about his means, further than that he seemed to spend a good bit of money. In short, what little they did know about him had come principally from the outside world, for Horace Crymes was singularly free from that every-day weakness—the narration of his own doings. It was not that he affected any secrecy, but he was habitually reserved and silent with men. With women it was different; beneath their influence the frost-bound springs of his conversation seemed to thaw, and those of them who had known him well were wont to observe that he was not only well read, but could be excessively entertaining. It seemed as if he did not consider it worth while to exert himself to titillate masculine understandings.

And yet people who thus judged Horace Crymes made a great mistake. There were few moves in his game of life that were not the result of cool calculation, and at times men had found him equally as fascinating as their wives or daughters, but such occasions were rare. He liked society. Society he held to be ruled by the women, if you wish to get on in it pay your court to them, and don't trouble your head about the men. They have little to give except shooting, and your fair friends will usually see you get a sufficiency of that.

It is the evening of Mrs. Charrington's garden-party, and the Major is sitting over the fire in his own quarters lost in thought. He has dined at mess, and it is needless to say has made no allusion to Calvert's rather impertinent ruse, not that he has at all forgotten it; there never was a man less likely to forget anything of the kind, but the Major holds that such social amenities should be reciprocated in similar fashion, and even amongst ladies Horace Crymes is considered a dangerous man to play tricks with, he having more than once displayed a most unforgiving memory for former slights when his opportunity came. But at present he is turning over a much more elaborate scheme in his mind, wherein vengeance on the two culprits is a very minor detail.

"Yes," he muttered, pulling rather hard at his cigar, as men are wont when solving some of those abstruse problems anent 'ways and means,' which are the lot of most of us, "I suppose it must come to that pretty speedily—a little sooner or later won't make much difference. I've one pull, thanks to having learnt to hold my tongue early in life; nobody has an idea of what difficulties I am in. It's bad enough to be hard up, but only let *your* world know it too, and you're dead broke before you can turn round. It's a pity these fellows (he meant his brother officers) know anything about my connection with the Turf. When you contemplate matrimony it goes against you; fathers-in-law never appreciate that connection. I kept it as dark as I could, too, but it's a babbling world we live in, and men don't wait for their death-beds 'to babble of green fields' that grow white rails and a winning-post.

"Hum! now to reckon things up; first, is Mrs. Charrington right about that Aysgarth girl? Is she a prize worth laying siege to? secondly, how far would she herself really help me? A woman's co-operation is valuable if you can trust her; the danger in my case is when it comes to the point Mrs. Charrington may regard me as somewhat too much her own property to resign, and if she takes that view, well," and here he emitted a cloud of smoke from under his moustache, "it will be deuced awkward. She's safe to know more about me than I think, and will invent it if she doesn't. A woman always does under such circumstances. Lastly, I wonder how far Miss Aysgarth is interested in that fellow Calvert; that there is some sort of understanding between them that dance business this afternoon showed; however, that don't go for much. It only means he has got the best of the start."

A knock at the door interrupted his reverie, and in obedience to his sharp "Come in," a wiry, hard-featured little man entered the room, closed the door behind him, and made a respectful bow.

"Well, Tom, what is it?" inquired the

Major. "I suppose you have fetched the grey horse home. How do you like him?"

"He's a good-looking nag enough," replied the new-comer. "We've had better, although I'll not deny we've had worse. I thought, sir, you'd like to know he'd arrived all right, and I wanted to see you about what sort of work I'm to give him."

Mr. Thomas Blundell conceived it his duty to disparage any horse, with the buying of which he had not been in some way concerned. Crymes had picked him up in a racing stable, from which he was on the verge of being discharged, on account of some suspicion as to his honesty, and appointed him his stud groom. A dangerous experiment that would probably have resulted in failure with most men, but in the Major's hands had turned out well so far. In the first place, there was no such temptation to turn rogue as there had been in his former situation, and in the second, Mr. Blundell had a wholesome appreciation of his new master's astuteness, and a strong conviction that he was dangerous to play tricks with.

"We may have had better, no doubt," returned the Major, "because at present I can't say I know much about The Cid, but I rather fancy we shall find him a pretty good horse. Put him in training at once. I mean to run him in the Regimental Cup just to see what he's like. I shall be disappointed if he's not good enough for the Grand Military in the spring."

"We can very soon see what chance this Cid has for the Regimental Cup, sir. Old Cockatoo can tell us all about that. He won it two years ago, and there's not likely, as I've heard of, to be anything much better in the field than what he beat then. None of the gentlemen have been buying anything of much account. That second charger of Mr. Harperley's is smart, but they've had him fiddling about so long in the school, he's most likely forgot how to gallop."

"You're right, Tom, the school may make 'em handy, but it don't make them quick. He'll not be dangerous this year."

Although Mr. Blundell at present had simply the care of his master's chargers and hunters, he still hankered after his old vocation. As Chrysippus considered the cause of cocks was cock-fighting, so Mr. Blundell apprehended the cause of horses was horse-racing. To get a horse into condition, and then not at least match him against something or other, was, in his eyes, a lamentable waste of oats, time, and talent. Hunting was all very well, but only as a means to an end; useful for schooling, and also for obtaining the necessary qualifications to run in stakes fictitiously supposed to be designed for horses habitually ridden to hounds; but the real salt of existence, the acme of human felicity, was in Mr. Blundell's eyes a big match, with about 10lb. the best of your opponent. His being allowed to train Cockatoo, a *boná fide* hunter, was the one white stone in his career since he had entered the Major's service, some five years back, so that the prospect of once more preparing two or three horses for a race of any sort was excessively exhilarating to Mr. Blundell.

"And you'll put them together—I mean old Cockatoo and this Cid—before the race, I suppose, sir? As likely as not the old horse will prove the best of the two," added Tom, in tones of disparagement.

"Certainly! I shall enter the pair, try them, and may be run both."

"Run both, sir?"

"I shall, perhaps, do so; and now, Tom, you've got your orders, and know as much as I mean to tell you at present."

Mr. Blundell took the hint, and with a respectful "Good night, sir," made his exit. "The Major's clever," he muttered, as he descended the stairs; "but he's hard, aye, hard as Brazilian nuts. He'll give me my orders, but never show me a bit of his hand. What does he want to run two for? What's his little game in that? Means to gammon them, I suppose, as to which is the genuine pea. It will go hard if I don't know before the day, and if I don't, why, I'll perhaps choose it for him. It's to be hoped our interests may be identical," and Mr. Blundell, as he emerged into the barrack square, winked confidentially at the gas-lamp, in due recognition of the comicality of his idea.

The Major took two or three rapid turns up and down the room as his servitor left him. "What has put it into my head to win this steeple-chase!" he exclaimed; "pique! by heavens, nothing else. I won it two years ago just to show that I could win it—that's all very well for once, but I don't habitually play for the gallery—there is no money to talk of to be made over it. Besides, to clean out one's own regiment don't sound well. It would be buying money too dear. No, it is pique, nothing else, that has determined me to take the Cup this year. Calvert shan't have it if I can prevent it. A few hours ago, and he was welcome to it as far as I was concerned. Now I have determined to cut his comb, and, if he is in earnest about Miss Aysgarth, so am I, and he need never count he has done with Horace Crymes till he has placed the ring on her finger. I'll not stand being thrown over by a country chit like that, more especially when she embodies money, which at this present moment it is my special vocation to wed. No, I am sorry to interfere with Pyramus and Thisbe; but, as I want Thisbe myself, I am afraid Pyramus must become the victim of circumstances."

* * * * *

Curiously enough, in another barrack room, not very far off, a somewhat similar scene was being enacted. Cis Calvert had, after the manner of his rival, left mess early, and strolled back to his quarters to indulge in day-dreams, visions of brighter hue than those which had mingled with the smoke wreaths around the Major's head. Never had Miss Aysgarth been so gracious to him as this day, and Cis was conscious that he had no whit neglected the occasion. He had danced a good deal with her, he had sat out with her more than once, and had assumed an air of proprietorship that had been prettily submitted to on her part. He had cloaked her and put her into the carriage, and fancied when he pressed her hand warmly at saying adieu that it was faintly returned. He was quite aware that he had been making as fierce love to the girl all the afternoon as the opportunity admitted, and his heart swelled with triumph at the idea that his attentions had been in no wise rebuffed. Cis was very earnest in his wooing, and was now counting up the probabilities of his success. He had never been told that Miss Aysgarth was an heiress. He had not the advantage of Mrs. Charrington for a friend, and so was happily ignorant of what would have seemed to him only an extra obstacle to the fulfilment of his desires. Still he did know that the girl was the only daughter of a man reputed wealthy, and that it was quite likely he might regard a captain of dragoons, with only five hundred a-year besides his pay, as no fitting match for his daughter, and yet he felt no disposition to undervalue himself. Let him only win Annie Aysgarth herself, and he thought he would speedily succeed in wringing her father's consent. Do not think that there was any tinge of conceit about Cis Calvert, though he had some of the swagger essential to the class he belonged to. You cannot incite men to wear caps on one side and wax their moustaches without putting a certain amount of that into them, but Cis was by no means unduly confident about his present love-chase; indeed, until to-day he had experienced dire misgivings as to what advance he had made in the lady's good graces. In short, it was only the fortunate result of his first audacity that afternoon that had emboldened him to make such severe running as he had done. But the thread of his meditations is cut short by a sharp tap at the door, and hardly waiting for his response, Harry Harperley enters.

For a minute or two Cis regrets bitterly he has neglected to slip down the latch, but to the brother of the object of our devotion much toleration is existent; and then again, albeit he had not desired that his day-dreams should be broke in upon, Cis really likes the boy for his own sake. Still, wrapped in his own ecstatic vision, he feels that he cannot quite sympathize with

Harry's perpetual lament over *his* lost love, and he knows that the Cornet is about to indulge in jeremiads over the bad luck which has prevented his becoming the proprietor of The Cid. He noticed that night at dinner the boy's wine did him no good, his grievance was rankling in his breast, and he gulped down his liquor in saturnine fashion, and refused to be comforted, as men do under serious affliction, such as finding the bride they hope to win is engaged to somebody else, or that the bookmaker whom for once they have landed for 'a thousand to thirty' is hopelessly insolvent.

"Sit down, young-un," exclaimed Cis; "put one of those big cigars *in* your mouth, and for heaven's sake don't let anything concerning that grey horse *out* of it. It's rough, I admit, and I heartily wish the governor had got there before Crymes, but he didn't. So there's no more to be said about it."

"Ah, well! you do admit it is an awful

sell," exclaimed Harry. "I know that horse is safe to win the Regimental Cup. He's about as handsome as any I ever saw, and Mappin declares that, to the best of his belief, he's as good as he looks."

"I don't say he won't, but remember, all racing is a game of great uncertainty, more especially steeple-chasing. I don't myself think if he finds him very good that Crymes will run him. We know he has horses with which he could probably beat anything the rest of us have, and he never spoils sport by running them. Last year, though of course he subscribed, he didn't even start one, and during the four that he has been in the regiment he has never won it but the once, and then with a most legitimate hunter. His old white horse, Cockatoo, remember, cannot be counted more, though no doubt very good of his class. I am not quite convinced, indeed, that he can beat Red Lancer. I only bought him just before that race, and he was so utterly out of condition that it would have been absurd to start him. He'll go this year though, and settle that question."

"What do you think of that brown horse Mappin has?" added young Harperley, wriggling restlessly in his chair. "The governor says I may have him if I like, and recommends me to take him, as I can't have the grey."

"I agree with your father, and think you can't do better. Now, for heaven's sake, let us talk no more horse, I'm sick of it for the present."

Harry opened his eyes in wide amazement. The Regimental Cup was to him at present what the Derby was to the London world the week before Epsom in those days, an all-absorbing event, before which the upsetting of thrones on the Continent faded into utter insignificance. He could, as a schoolboy, recollect Surplice breaking the magic spell at Doncaster in '48 by winning the double event, and the enthusiasm it occasioned; but I am afraid, like many of riper years, was hardly cognisant of Louis Phillippe's precipitate arrival on our shores. What could Cis want to talk about? Was there a nobler subject of conversation than the horse? He had never read Pope, or he would have greatly derided the famous line, "The proper study for mankind is man," and pronounced authoritatively that the poet had never been in Yorkshire.

Still, whatever might be the subject his host wished to introduce, he certainly was in no hurry to begin, as can be well understood, for, in reality, he merely wished to continue the love-musings which his self-invited guest had so rudely interrupted.

The Cornet, damped by Calvert's taciturnity and the embargo on a monody, regarding the loss of 'The Cid,' was about to exchange the dulness of his present situation for 'pastures new,' when a tap at the door arrested his attention, and he sank back in the chair from which he had half risen. The new-comer was Trooper Timothy Murphy, bâtman and master of the horse to Captain Cecil Calvert of her Majesty's —th Lancers.

Tim, as he was familiarly called, was a thorough good specimen of the Irish soldier. A spare, muscular man, standing somewhat over 5ft. 9in. in his boots, with red hair, light grey eyes, upturned nose, and somewhat large mouth; he looked the very incarnation of fun and good-humour, but there was a glint in the eye and a twitch about the corners of the mouth at times that would have told a physiognomist that Tim Murphy was no fool.

He had been Calvert's henchman now for some years, and his faith in 'the masther' was as unbounded as his attachment to him.

"Halloa, Murphy!" exclaimed young Harperley, welcoming any relief to the oppressive silence into which they had subsided, "what's the row?"

"'Deed, there's nothing the matter,

Misther Harperley. I just looked in on the Masther for a moment, but, as I see yer honour's engaged, I'll just come again in the morning."

"What is it?" inquired Calvert, shortly. "You've been on pass, of course, I know, but it is pretty well time you were over at your barrack-room."

"I was going there straight, but I saw a light in your honour's rooms, so I made bould to come up. It's about that black 'atomy ye bought a fortnight ago, sir. There's been a fellow questioning me about him in York to-day, and sorra a bit I can understand his maning."

"What did he say?" inquired Cis.

"'Your name's Tim Murphy,' says he.

"'They call me that mostly,' says I.

"'Captain Calvert's groom,' says he.

"'You're a divil at guessing,' says I.

"'Ah, 'twas your master, then, bought that half ton of bones done up in horse-hair, old Mappin called a hunter.'

" 'And why not?' says I, 'shure's he's going into high farming, and it's bones they swear by just now.'

" 'Bones are on the rise,' says he, grinning, 'may be he'd like to turn a five pound note on his bargain.'

" 'Och, niver a one of me knows,' says I; 'but an' he wor wise he'd give you that just to take him off the premises.'

" 'Well,' he says softly, 'you see he was sold out of a family in which he was a great favourite, under peculiar circumstances; they're a bit sore at his loss, and would give a thrifle to get him back.'

" 'Just so; their grandmother's favourite hack, I understand. Troth I riverence the feeling; they don't like heirlooms like that going out of the family.'

" 'That's it,' he said. 'Captain Calvert's a good man, no doubt; but the poor crather's too ould for hunting, and so is no use to him. It'd be murther to attempt it.'

" 'An' it's turning the poor baste out to end his days in pace, you'd be doing with him?' I asked.

" 'My excellent friend, you've just hit it.' Those were his very words, your honour. 'He's past work, and we can't bear the idea of his being called on to do it.'

" 'Ah! well. If the masther's willing to part with him, it'll be a proud day when I bring him back to ye. Where will I be inquiring after you?'

" 'When your masther's tired of his bargain,' says he, 'you can just ask for Isham Boggs at the Punchbowl Tavern in Stonegate. They know me there, good day.' And off he walked with never another word."

"What sort of looking man was he?" inquired Calvert at the end of this history.

" 'Deed he looked more like a Methody parson down on his luck than anything else. Most of the colour of his face had settled in his nose, and he'd a fair case for an action against his laundress av his linen went to the wash reg'lar."

"And what about the horse, Murphy?" inquired Harry Harperley, who had listened to this conversation with the greatest interest.

"Well, sir, he's a good doer, but his oats seem to do him no good. I can't get him to carry any flesh. The boys down at Mappin's tould me he was a grate lepper, but I've never tried him meeself."

"All right, that'll do," said Calvert sharply, "good night." And in obedience to the mandate Mr. Murphy took his departure.

"What do you think of this?" inquired the Cornet eagerly as the door closed.

"Think, my dear Harry, that I have got an old horse worth rather more than I thought he was; that's all at present, but I think further that I am very tired, and it is high time to go to bed. So I exhort you to follow Tim's example, and take your departure."

A request with which the Cornet immediately complied, walking back to his quarters much exercised in his understanding.

CHAPTER IV.

A DINNER AT THE FIRS.

MISS AYSGARTH was under no delusion as to what had taken place between herself and Cis Calvert at the garden-party. She was a young woman, remember, and not a girl; the distinction is really very great, although the terms are constantly looked upon as synonymous. At eighteen a girl *fancies* herself in love more often than not, but at twenty-four she should make no mistake on the subject. She knows thoroughly then, if she has any common sense in her, what she takes a man for—whether it is for position, a comfortable home, or from pure simple love of him.

Annie Aysgarth was quite aware that Cis had shown her very marked attention, she was equally aware that she had deliberately encouraged him, and that the world generally were also cognizant of the fact. She was, as before said, a clear-headed young lady, whom flattery had never imposed upon; singularly free from coquetry, a weapon of her sex for which she had a supreme disdain, and, moreover, perfectly heart-free up to these last few days. Annie Aysgarth felt that it behoved her to think in sober earnest now whether she cared enough for this man to marry him. She never doubted but that he would ask her. Too proud to condescend to the game of flirtation herself, it never occurred to her that any man would dare play that with her, and in Cis Calvert's case, as we know, she was perfectly justified in this assumption.

It was the more imperative, she considered, because on the Friday, and it was now Wednesday, her father had a large dinner-party, intended to resolve itself into a small dance later on. Captain Calvert was amongst those invited, and Annie felt that she must be prepared to answer this question definitely at any moment. She had no idea of keeping any lover of hers shilly-shallying. She would place her hand in his, and own she loved him with all her heart, or gently tell him he was scarce justified in mistaking her kindly feeling towards him for more than friendliness. She knew she could not honestly say the latter now to Cis Calvert, but it was still possible to say him nay. She had after all seen but little of him when she came to think of it. He was not the ideal she had pictured to herself; no, Major Crymes she was bound to confess more represented that; but still, the fact remained—she rather disliked the Major, and had more than a suspicion that she cared for gay, light-hearted, *insouciant* Cis a great deal more than she ought. Miss Aysgarth had indulged in visions of a hero of god-like intellect and Apollo-like physique, such as is seldom to be met with in this work-a-day world, as the man she would bow down to and worship. Being in the main a sensible young woman she never expected to meet him exactly, but she deemed that the man she married should be at all events a faint copy of that ideal. She could not delude herself into the idea that Cis Calvert represented him in any shape; he was only of medium height, instead of the six feet she had fixed upon as imperative. He was light in complexion, when he should have been dark; tolerably good-looking, but not at all suggestive of Apollo; a practical, sensible man, but showing no sign of high intellectual power, and yet she felt she loved him. Why? Ah that will be a difficult question for woman, aye, or man, too, for the matter of that, to answer till the hour-glass of this world is turned for the last time.

But did she love Cis well enough to leave her father for him?—that was now the great question in her mind. Very, very passionate was the love Annie bore her step-father, and none knew better than she what a terrible gap it would make in his life. Convinced that it was for her happiness that the man of her choice was an honourable upright gentleman, and she knew that her father would smother his own feelings, nor permit her to feel by sign or word the wrench it was for him. She had done her duty by him, as he by her; she was loth to leave him, but Julian Harperley was, she felt, the last man to exact the sacrifice of her whole life to his comfort; she knew her step-father better than that. Did she love Cis Calvert well enough for this—to leave her own people for his sake?—and Annie felt that was a question not to be determined lightly. She knew that she loved him, she thought that he loved her, but then did he? Glance and gesture had told her so, but the avowal of his love was as yet unspoken, and so, spite of her shrewd, clear understanding, the girl was tossed here and there in her imaginings, like the veriest love-lorn maiden of sweet seventeen. In love-making, as in racing, the fierce exultation of winning is as nothing to the fervid excitement of the yet undecided contest.

Coming in from a ride with her father on the Thursday she found Captain Calvert's card upon the table. A slight tremour ran through her frame at sight of it. Men do not usually call at a house the day before they are engaged to dine there, and she thought had she been at home she might have been asked that very question about which her mind was as yet undetermined. More made up, perhaps, than she was aware of, as is the case with most of us in our moments of indecision, demonstrated by our weakness for begging that advice from our friends which we so rarely follow.

In these more enlightened days, when

people are told off to their respective chairs, the hostess has a chance of mixing the social salad to the best of her ability, which the old scramble for seats utterly forbade. Then various readjustment was often necessary to prevent all the vinegar collecting in one place, or in other words, the more discordant elements finding themselves in closest proximity. But it also had this advantage—it offered great opportunities to the audacious, who often succeeded in obtaining the coveted position by a little readiness and *sang froid.* Calvert, on the eventful Friday, knew that he could not hope to take in the lady of the house; there was sure to be some dignitary to claim that privilege, but he was determined to be as close to her as possible. No sooner, then, was dinner announced than he tucked the young lady committed to his charge under his arm, silenced some faint remonstrances she made on the question of precedence with the suave remark that he 'always went in with the Dukes,' and promptly followed Julian Harperley's footsteps. He was successful in his design, and found himself next Miss Aysgarth when the party had finally settled down into their places. He had no reason to complain of the manner in which that young lady received this arrangement; on the contrary, she smiled her approval of it; but the achievement of a *tête-à-tête* at a dinner-party must be always due to fortunate circumstances. The flaxen-haired young lady who was Calvert's temporary partner had a leaning for soldiers, and was not at all disposed to allow the light dragoon fate had consigned her to neglect his duty. Mr. Charrington, on the other hand, conceived it his duty to entertain Miss Aysgarth, so that Cis had little chance of pleading his cause.

It was a largish dinner-party, and casting his eye down the table, somewhat to his astonishment, Calvert saw that Major Crymes was seated next Mrs. Charrington. There was nothing really odd in his being there; if not intimate he had certainly dined at 'The Firs' before; the only thing singular about it was that he had never mentioned he was invited when Cis had alluded to the party the night before at mess. Still, the Major was not given to publish his movements to the world he lived in, so there was not much in that, and yet Cis Calvert kept on wondering what the deuce Crymes was doing there. Once he saw Mrs. Charrington glance his way, and then turn and address some observation to her neighbour, to which the Major returned a negative shake of the head. What could Mrs. Charrington have to say about him, thought Cis, and his reply to an observation of his fair companion was so palpably at random, that the nymph of the flaxen locks momentarily doubted whether the champagne had not been too liberally handed about. Cis indeed was in a state of nervous excitability. His was one of those peculiarly high-strung temperaments to whom suspense is of all the most intolerable. These are the men who before the fight you foretell will utterly lose their heads, and who, the fray once commenced, display a coolness and presence of mind perfectly marvellous. Cis had made up his mind to put his fate to the test this night, and chafed at everything that delayed the desired explanation. This reckless dragoon deemed apparently that love speeches with the soup, a proposal with the *entrées*, bless you my children with the cheese, and the health of the bride and bridegroom as the decanters made their first circuit, was the way the giving in marriage was ordinarily conducted in this country. No man ever was more destined to be corrected on this point, or have the story of Jacob's servitude more pointedly recalled to his memory.

Miss Aysgarth bends her head, the ladies rise, and as he holds the door open Cis reflects ruefully that he has exchanged barely a dozen sentences with the enchantress, despite the audacious *coup de main* that had placed him near her. He turns him again moodily to the table, and becomes speedily involved in that all-absorbing topic to a Yorkshireman in September, 't Leger. The first half of the month they discuss fiercely what is to win it, during the second they are wont to argue with no little asperity as to what ought to have won it. Nearly every man at the table had seen it run, and had had his bet upon the race, and there were those who still clung to the belief that the Whitewall horse was out of trim, refusing to recognize that his Epsom success was due to Frank Butler, the state of the ground, and luck, and that the king of the year was Lord Exeter's mighty chesnut, who, albeit ridden by 'the post-boy,' fairly smothered 'Daniel,' in spite of the assistance of the crack jockey of the day. Others there were who shook their heads over Songstress, and muttered grimly she would run a very different mare when wanted, so that there was much Turf argument going on round the banker's table. Crymes sat, as was his custom, taciturn in the midst of all this racing talk, into which Cis Calvert had plunged wildly. A looker-on would have pronounced the one man devoted to the Turf, while he would have deemed the other a somewhat bored listener to a discussion which in no wise interested him, and this was precisely the conclusion Julian Harperley came to as he sat watching his guests in indolent fashion. No more erroneous deduction was of course ever drawn, as the two men's betting volumes would have shown, could the banker but have seen them. They had both lost their money; but, whereas Calvert's cheque for a hundred would more than have covered his liabilities, the Major's were of a kind likely to necessitate intimate relations with the tribes, and heartfelt thanksgiving that they were not all lost.

'Still waters run deep,' is one of the

aphorisms I believe in. Your garrulous Don Juan has, usually, scarce courage to kiss his cousin under the mistletoe, and the way a man who has lost five pounds over an Ascot Meeting will fill the walls of his club with querulous and ear-piercing lamentation over his awful luck is a common, though sorry sight to witness. Now those who are 'plungers' either in love or racing are usually first heard of in the journals, and much to the surprise of their friends.

"You must excuse us, Major Crymes," remarked the banker at last, "but you know to us Yorkshiremen Doncaster races are a solemn festival, and to guard the Leger from the Southron the first duty of the many-acred county. This year we have been beaten on our own dunghill, we are all a little sore in consequence, and would fain explain away our defeat."

"Ah! I fancy the best horse won, though, from what I saw," replied Crymes, rousing himself from a reverie into which he had fallen. He had never taken very much notice of Miss Aysgarth before, but he had watched her pretty closely at dinner, and he was rather astonished to think so handsome a girl had not attracted his attention sooner. He was more determined than ever to win her for his wife if he could. He was *bonâ fide* struck with the girl. He wanted money; it was getting time to settle down and have done with soldiering, and then there was private pique. He detested Calvert — he could hardly have said why—still he did. Few of us can account for these instinctive dislikes. Then he could not forget the way Miss Aysgarth had thrown him over at the garden party. Absurd to think a girl's caprice could have such an effect on a man not even in love with her, but so it was. To paraphrase the words of the preacher, 'all is vanity;' 'master passion of mankind,' as Sheridan pronounced it.

"We are all looking forward with interest to your steeple-chases. My boy especially is enthusiastic about that grey you bought of Mappin, and declares the Regimental Cup is at your mercy. I presume you will run him?"

"Yes, I think so, Mr. Harperley. I don't know much about the horse as yet, and it will be an excellent opportunity to try him. By the way, next Wednesday is our nomination night, and we have got some men coming to dine. If you would give me the pleasure of your company I should be very pleased."

"I shall be delighted," rejoined the banker. "I've no doubt you will have a cheery party, and that there will be no end of chaff over the nominations. Pass the sherry, please. Any one down there for a white-wash?"

In the drawing-room Annie Aysgarth busies herself about her guests, flitting softly from one to another as the occasion prompted. She was making conversation with an old friend of her father's when Cis Calvert's name fell upon her ears.

"No, my dear," replied Mrs. Charrington, in answer to some question of Cis's flaxen-haired dinner partner, "I don't know much of Captain Calvert."

"Well, he can hardly be deaf at his age, but I declare he is the most absent man I ever encountered."

"Which means, Lottie, he wasn't thinking of you. Well, comfort yourself, he'd no business to. Let us hope his thoughts were where they ought to be."

"And where is that, I should like to know, Mrs. Charrington, unless with the lady he is taking care of?"

"Well, when he is going to take care of another for life, you must make allowances for his being a little distrait. If he was thinking of the cousin he is going to marry, you must not be hard upon him. Stupid, I admit, with you by his side, and shows a want of adaptability most unusual in a dragoon."

Not a word of this conversation was lost upon Miss Aysgarth, and she set her little white teeth hard, and her face flushed as she recalled how she had accustomed herself of late to think of this man. Was Mrs. Charrington's story true? She felt that she must get at the truth somehow before she slept. The sharp surgery of the truth was better than the incessant pin-pricks of suspicion. She was aware of Mrs. Charrington's besetting weakness, but she did not know that all the same we cannot help giving some credence to unreliable testimony when our feelings are concerned. Mrs. Charrington was not wilfully lying upon this occasion. She was only telling what she had heard after her own fashion. One of the stray guests at her garden party, brought there by one of her friends, had observed—"I see you have got a countryman of mine here, Cis Calvert.

We used to think he would marry his cousin Kate, but he's still a bachelor." Mrs. Charrington had retold this with unusual accuracy—that is, for her.

And now the gentlemen gradually stream in from the dining-room, and amongst the foremost was Cis Calvert, bent upon the achievement of that conversation which he had so failed to procure at dinner. But Miss Aysgarth was apparently in no mood to lend herself to this design. The sunshine of the dining-room had died away, and to his amazement Cis met with a somewhat chilly reception. The girl could not help it; she knew Mrs. Charrington's habit of exaggeration; she did not in her heart believe that her lover could trifle with her in this fashion, and yet for the life of her she could not avoid showing in her manner that this story had laid hold of her imagination. To have taken offence on the one side about that which does not admit of explanation, and on the other to be conscious of the offending, but innocent of the manner of it, has resulted many times in a good lasting quarrel, but is sure to be productive of a game of cross purposes, to say the least of it. Cis felt that he had unexpectedly lost the key of the situation, and marvelled much as to what the arraignment against him might be, while Miss Aysgarth felt dissatisfied with herself, indignant with Mrs. Charrington, and angry with her lover for not at once vindicating himself in her eyes, regardless of the fact that he could by no possibility be aware of what had been alleged concerning him.

To one as well versed in the ways of women as Horace Crymes, it was little likely that Miss Aysgarth's change of manner should pass unnoticed. He had no idea of the cause, but it was plain to him that something had gone wrong between her and Calvert. That lovers' quarrels are rivals' opportunities no man knew better; he was fairly in the field now, and determined to make the most of the chance with which fortune had favoured him. Should he only progress as far in the young lady's good graces as he had contrived to do in the good will of her father, he thought he should not be doing a very bad evening's work to begin upon. Acting upon this idea, the Major made his way at once to Miss Aysgarth's side, and at once engaged her in conversation. As she had herself said, Horace Crymes was a good talker, but though he did his best to interest her, it was apparent that his fair companion's attention was somewhat astray. He understood all that, and was nothing daunted by it. She might not listen to him now, but that was no reason she should not do so a little later. A bad start he knew, from former experience, may be recovered, like most things, by patience and perseverance, and he possessed that great virtue of knowing how to wait. Not only did he succeed in somewhat monopolizing the young hostess, but when the dancing commenced he led her forth for the quadrille.

Exercised severely by the lady of their love, men either affect to console themselves with a counter-attraction or sulk. Cis was somewhat too hard hit for the former, so he betook himself to the latter line of conduct. He did not, of course, stalk about like a Manfred in private life, nor altogether drop the mask society demands of us all, but he wandered about rather vaguely, complained slightly of headache, and showed no disposition to dance with any one. Inwardly he was anathematizing Horace Crymes and woman's fickleness, with an intention that would have been highly estimated at Red Gulch or any other of the Colorado mining stations.

But Miss Aysgarth herself was not having altogether what is called a good time of it. No sooner was she conscious of the effect of her displeasure on her victim—and she watched him closely from those eyes at the back of her head which all women appear to possess—than she felt a little penitent for her behaviour, and remembered that she had pronounced sentence without waiting to hear if the culprit had anything to say in his defence. Then she reflected that she must at all events know whether Mrs. Charrington's statement had any foundation; and how was she to know that if she kept the only person from whom it was possible to learn the true state of the case at arm's length. Her resolve was speedily taken, and no sooner did the quadrille come to an end than, with her sweetest smile, she asked Major Crymes to take her across to Captain Calvert. "He is really neglecting his duties shamefully," she added, laughing, "and I must scold him." That done, and much more to the surprise of Cis than his rival, the Major was dismissed with a saucy little nod, and Miss Aysgarth and her lover were face to face.

"How is it you are not dancing, Captain Calvert? I really cannot allow you to remain idle. We are not, sad to say, so bountifully supplied with cavaliers that such a knight of the ball-room as yourself can be excused his devoir."

"I trust I am something better than that," rejoined Cis grimly, "but I did not know that my services were required. I am at your disposal, Miss Aysgarth; with whom shall I dance?"

"With me, I think, if it is not imposing too much on your good-nature," rejoined the young lady demurely. "You see," she continued, as she took his arm, "I should like to be one of the first to offer my congratulations."

"About what?" inquired Cis curtly.

"I am told you are engaged to be married."

"And is there any one in this room so capable of contradicting the report?" rejoined Cis, in a passionate whisper. "What nonsense you may have heard I can't tell; but that the question I tremble to put has yet to be answered you know as well as I do."

"But they say you're engaged to your cousin," faltered Miss Aysgarth.

"Do you suppose if there had been the faintest ground for such a report I should have dared to speak to you as I did at the Charringtons'? Do you hold me such a hound, Annie, that I could make love to you while I was engaged to another? If I don't rank higher in your esteem than that, I fear there is small hope for me."

"I didn't say I believed it," stammered Miss Aysgarth.

"Do you believe I love you?" whispered

Cis. "You must have known that, Annie, for weeks. As for the story you have heard about my cousin—well—she and I have always been real good cousins, nothing more. I vowed when I came here to-night to ask you one question. You know what it is. What answer am I to take away with me? Am I to leave The Firs supremely happy, or sadly regret the day I first saw the walls of York."

The girl looked up into his face, inquiringly.

"Can you love me well enough to be my wife?" said Cis, in a low whisper.

Once more she looked him steadily in the face. Then a slight quiver played round her mouth, her eyes dropped, a little hand stole into his, and she answered softly, "Yes."

CHAPTER V.

THE NOMINATIONS FOR THE CUP.

It was a gala night at the mess of Her Majesty's —th Lancers, and the old room, scene of many a wild revel, glittered with plate and wax lights. These were the last days of the army of the great Duke, remember, of the veritable inheritors of the Peninsula traditions; when the infantry had a quiet contempt for Brown Bess as a firearm, but a mighty belief in the efficacy of the bayonet; when the cavalry held that any square of foot soldiers not British was to be broken; when the joints were placed on the table in all their barbaric splendour, and dinners *à la Russe* were as yet in the womb of time; when men not only could drink port, but did, by pailfuls, and toned it down afterwards with a grilled bone and a trifle of whisky punch. How they stood it is a mystery, but the veterans that are left should have some consolation in the gout that now mostly afflicts them when they reflect that they *did* earn it.

The nominations for the Regimental Cup are to be published to-night, and, although pretty well known already, still the —th have determined to have a party to give a little *éclat* to the official announcement. Julian Harperley is there by Major Crymes's invitation, not that Calvert troubles himself much on that point since his last evening at The Firs. He feels now that he is an accepted lover, and any transient uneasiness he might have felt about the Major is a thing of the past. Mr. Charrington is there—shrewd, sharp, and combative as ever. Many other guests are there besides these two, who, as they have no bearing on this narrative, it would be useless to particularize. In fact, it was a full house, and to those conversant with the habits of those apparently *nonchalant* light dragoons, there was presage of an exceeding wet evening. It was the custom of the corps; they were all so quiet and silky to start with that the stranger within their gates could never dream of 'the high jinks' the evening was destined to terminate in. So insidiously did they steal on their victims as a rule, that temperate men found themselves drinking burnt brandy punch and joining in tumultuous choruses hours after the wives of their bosoms had expected them home, and with no idea that they had exceeded a bottle of claret.

Dinner passed off pleasantly enough, as with good wine, decent cooking, and cheery hosts, a dinner is bound to do, and then having drunk 'the Queen,' there was a lull in the conversation while the pay-master, who took this duty upon himself, proceeded to read out the entries for the regimental races; for, besides the Cup, there was a Farmers' Plate and also a Challenge Vase, open to all members of the York and Ainsty Hunt, but the Cup was the event upon which interest chiefly centred. One curious thing about such races as this is, that they are apt to look a foregone conclusion and result in a most unexpected 'turn up.' In a regiment every one knows, or fancies he knows, all about everybody else's horses, and so imagines it is very easy to say what will probably win, quite forgetting that amateur training and amateur riding are apt to upset all calculations at times. Now the Major's new purchase was of course no secret. They had all seen and admired The Cid, and the prevalent belief was that there was nothing in the regiment capable of beating that grand-looking grey, therefore no little astonishment was manifested when it was found that besides The Cid the Major had also nominated Cockatoo.

Could it be that the new purchase was not quite so good as he looked? but surely he must be better than old Cockatoo, who, besides, had incurred a 10lb. penalty for having already won the Cup, and who had won with not much in hand either.

"You don't seem to put quite so much faith in The Cid as Mappin does," remarked Julian Harperley. "Running a second string looks as if you—"

"Didn't know much about him," interposed Crymes; "just so. I believe him to be the best of the pair considerably, but I don't know as yet, and I have seen too many handsome impostors in my time to trust to looks implicitly. All these fellows think I am safe to win the Cup with him—why? because Mappin, who wanted to sell the horse, said so. They know nothing more than he is a good-looking one."

"Hallo!" suddenly exclaimed a vivacious subaltern, named Radcliffe, "here's another case of second string. Cis Calvert's named a couple; here's Captain Calvert's chestnut horse, Red Lancer, and Captain Calvert's black horse, The Mumper. What's that?"

"You don't mean to say you've entered that skeleton you bought out of the hounds' mouths?" laughed another. "Never were dogs more defrauded of their just due than when you interfered between Mappin and his good intentions. He picked up that horse with a view of presenting him to the kennel."

"Never you mind, Strangford; The Mumper will very likely beat more than beat him. He's a bit poor, perhaps, but he may mend of that."

Mixed with all the chaff was no little surprise as to what could have induced Calvert to enter this new purchase. Some of his brother officers had not even seen it, and those that had wondered not a little what had made him buy such an old screw, for it was palpably an old horse that had done a lot of work in its time—well bred, no doubt, and not without some good points, but never likely to look like a gentleman's hunter, put what corn into him you would. Nobody was more astonished and excited about the entry of The Mumper than Harry Harperley. He had been present, as we know, in Calvert's room when Tim Murphy had reported his mysterious conversation with Isham Boggs. What had Cis found out about the horse since then that had determined him to run The Mumper for the Cup? He would have been much astonished if he had been told nothing; that the entering of The Mumper was due to the earnest entreaties of Tim Murphy, who had all an Irishman's passionate admiration for a grand jumper, and this he had ascertained the old horse to be; but then he had been sold to Cis with that character, and he could fairly have said with Crymes that his knowledge of his new purchase was simply what the horse-dealer had chosen to tell him.

As the claret circulated, discussion waxed warm about the various chances of the competitors for the Cup, and it speedily came to pass that opinions were not only emphatically expressed, but boldly backed by the disputants, until at last, amidst the Babel of chaff, Strangford announced his intention of opening a book on the forthcoming race, if only the owner of the favourite would give him a start.

"Now, Major," he exclaimed, "set the market; they have made The Cid first favourite down here. What shall I lay you? Take my whole book, and let me lay you two hundred to one."

"No, thank you, Strangford. I'll take two ponies for fun if you like; but I tell you all, that I believe The Cid to be a good horse, but as yet know nothing about him."

"It's a bet," rejoined Strangford sententiously. "Now, gentlemen, who wants to back one? I keep my own of course; Herodia runs for me."

The amateur bookmaker got plenty of custom for the next few minutes. All he had to lay about both The Cid and Red Lancer was rapidly appropriated, and then there came a lull.

"Pass the decanters, Radcliffe," cried the layer of odds. "Tho' business is slackening, thirst is on the increase. Won't anybody else back one?"

"Yes, I will," exclaimed young Harperley. "What against The Mumper?"

"Now look here, Cornet," retorted Strangford, with mock-solemnity, "this touching loyalty to your Captain is a thing beautiful to witness, and for which we must all both reverence and pity you, but you don't mean in earnest that you want to back that old plate-rack Cis found by the wayside the other day. His story of buying it of Mappin is of course apocryphal."

"What will you lay against The Mumper?" replied the boy doggedly.

"You can have two hundred to fifteen, if

you really do wish to make me a small present," was the reply.

"Done!" replied Harry Harperley. "I'll take that."

The other nodded assent, and noted it in his betting-book.

In the mean time an animated argument was going on at the other end of the table between Mr. Charrington and the Major. The master of Byculla Grange was combative and dogmatic by nature. It had struck him as singular that Crymes should have entered two grey horses, although for the matter of that old Cockatoo was grey now only by courtesy, and perhaps more for the sake of saying something than aught else, he proceeded to state that in this country he never knew a good horse of that colour. With the Arab it was different, but the English thorough-bred of that colour was never good for anything.

But he had caught rather a tartar in the Major. Crymes pointed out that all tradition of ballad and poetry was rather in favour of greys. "Did not the old hunting song say:

'And the best of the horses that galloped that day,
Was the Squire's Neck or Nothing, and that was a grey.'

"What about Chanticleer, did he not consider him a good horse?"

No, he did not. Chanticleer was much overrated, a mere handicap horse, and as for poetry, faugh! what did such men know about it? they put in whatever colour suited their rhyme.

"Well, you will see my greys run better than you give them credit for," replied Crymes, apparently wishing to drop the subject.

"Then I shall see what I don't in the least expect," rejoined Charrington testily. "Will you bet me fifty pounds that you win the Cup?"

"No, that would be to back my pair at

evens against the field, and I should look for a better price than that."

Now there had been a good lot of wine drunk, and Mr. Charrington was one of those men whose wine does them no good. It is so at times, instead of growing genial under the influence of the rosy god, thawing to their fellow-creatures, and beaming with amiability, we meet cantankerous creatures who become more morose with every bumper, who become argumentative and obstinate, who once having started a topic that threatens to be disagreeable, pursue it with a pertinacity that sets one's teeth on edge.

He sat sipping his port and looking moodily at a written list of entries in front of him. "I don't like greys," he said, "I don't believe in them. Now, Crymes, I'll give you a chance to back your opinion. Captain Calvert's got a couple entered as well as yourself; only his are decent-coloured Christian horses, not Pagan circus-looking animals like yours. Will you back your pair against his for fifty?"

"Yes; or five hundred either," retorted the Major, contemptuously.

"You can put the remainder of the five hundred down to me if you like," exclaimed Cis, no little nettled at the disparaging tone assumed by the Major.

Crymes looked a little astonished for a second, then replied, "As you like, Calvert. You had better have an even monkey, and I can bet Charrington an odd fifty, or a hundred besides, if he likes."

"You shall bet me a hundred, then," said the latter; "I don't believe in grey horses."

The Major nodded assent, and, having noted the two transactions, turned quietly to his guest. "I must apologize, Mr. Harperley. When I asked you to hear the nominations for our races I had no idea these fellows would turn the mess-room into a betting-ring. Pray don't say I encouraged them because I have been driven into backing my own horses. My bets were put down my throat, and my attempt to choke them off by offering a big wager has only recoiled on my own head. It is always a mistake amongst brother officers, and I am surprised at Calvert taking me up in that way."

Julian Harperley had heard vaguely that Crymes had a weakness for the Turf, still he knew from his son that the Major never bet or played cards for more than nominal stakes in the regiment, and he honestly considered that such wagering as had taken place had been none of his seeking, but had been thrust upon him by Charrington and Calvert. It might be a mistaken mode of putting an end to Charrington's persecution, but Julian Harperley believed that Crymes had honestly meant no more than to extinguish his assailant when he proffered him a heavy bet, and he did the Major no more than justice, he had never dreamt of being taken up, much less by Calvert. It did not much matter to him, he meant winning the Cup this year, and he most certainly meant also backing his horse to win him a good stake. It might as well be won in one place as another, and then he felt that there would be no little satisfaction in beating, and winning money, from Cis Calvert. He had made up his mind, and intended to make defeating Cis for the Cup only the prelude to defeating him for a much bigger stake. He did not know that Cis had already proved successful in that other event, nor would that to a man of Crymes's persistency be deemed conclusive.

"And so you've been backing The Mumper, young un," said Cis, as Harry Harperley lounged up to him in the ante-room, dinner being brought to a termination, and coffee and cigars at length arrived at. "What made you do that?"

"I thought if it was worth your while to

enter him, it was worth my while to take a long shot about him. You said the other night, you know, you fancied, from what Murphy told you, that you'd got hold of a better horse than you thought for."

"Yes; and I entered him to-night to gratify Murphy, who's sweet upon the horse, because he's discovered him to be 'a grand lepper.' I bought him on that account, thinking I might find him useful among those big fences up in the Ainsty country, but I know no more about him as yet. To-morrow I must ride over and see Mappin, and find out whether there's any history attached to the horse, where he picked him up, and whether he knew anything about him before he came into his hands."

By this time things had settled down into the ordinary groove of big mess parties. The elders and more decorous of those present were absorbed in a rubber, while the more tumultuous element had organized a loo, characterized chiefly by the boldness of the play. It is astonishing how keen men are to take 'miss,' who have the best part of a magnum of champagne inside them. When you begin 'unlimited' at a shilling it sounds playing for sugar-plums, but when the players take 'miss' freely it very soon becomes a considerably less innocent amusement. I don't mean that it quite means high play, but it is possible for people of moderate income to wake in the morning and feel they have been indulging in that diversion. Julian Harperley noticed that prominent at this table were his son and Cis Calvert. How they were faring he of course had no idea, as his whist engaged his attention for the most part. As for Mr. Charrington, who also formed one of the whist table, there was no getting him to abandon his crotchet. He had transferred his dislike to light colour in horses to light colour in cards, and declared there was nothing to be done in the red suits. He played quite mechanically the good old-fashioned game he was accustomed to (asking for trumps was amongst the undiscovered blessings of the century as yet), uninfluenced by the wine he had swallowed, but turn him from his whim you could not. He refused to have a bet on the odd trick if a red suit was trumps, and even when he held four by honours in diamonds declared there was no trusting a deceitful light colour or a grey horse; if they ever did win it was always when no one had backed them. When between the deals it was suggested to him such a thing had been known at Baden or Homburg as a run on the red, he retorted angrily, "It might be, but he had never seen it," which, as he had never visited either of those places, was an answer hardly to the point. In fact, excess of wine had a very singular effect upon Mr. Charrington; it always increased his natural obstinacy, and was very apt to find its outlet in leading him to take up some absurd idea. It was not often he transgressed, but this was generally the result of such transgression.

But the whist table breaks up, and it is time for the seniors to retire. As the Major bids his guest good night, he remarks in a low tone,

"Don't think, Mr. Harperley, we're a play regiment because you have seen a little betting amongst us to-night. I assure you we are nothing of the sort, and I have never seen the Cup call forth such wagering before. It's not our custom, believe me."

"No, no," replied the banker, "I don't think that. Charrington's obstinacy and Calvert's excitement were, I fancy, chiefly responsible for the events of the evening. Did you ever encounter such a mule as the former? Whenever he gets too much wine in him no idea is too preposterous for him to adopt, and you might as well try to dam Niagara as convince him that he is wrong."

"That I must endeavour to do on the 12th December," replied Crymes laughing. "Once more, good night."

"Fortune's rather favoured me to-night," mused the Major as he walked back to his quarters, "it's not much, but every point in the game counts, and I fancy in the eyes of our intended father-in-law Calvert and myself changed characters to-night. I think he would say if he was weighing us in the scales just now, Calvert's a gambler, Crymes is not. I wonder what made that old idiot Charrington make such a set at me; he surely cannot have the bad taste to be jealous!"

Now this was exactly, though unconscious of it, what Mr. Charrington was. As men often suffer from suppressed gout without understanding what is the matter with them, so Mr. Charrington had for years suffered from suppressed jealousy, and to a man of that temperament Mrs. Charrington gave much opportunity.

His theories read by this light, when wine threw the jealousy partially out, were not altogether so wild, being generally based on mad opposition to his wife's favourite at the time on some point or another. In this instance it had been grey horses.

"Get on your nag, Harry, as soon as this is over," said Cis Calvert the next day at morning stables, "and we'll ride over to Mappin's before lunch. I want to ask him whether he really does know anything about The Mumper more than he told me when I bought him. Don't fancy, please, I think I've got a phenomenon; but, as he is entered for the Cup, I should like to know if he's got any chance; more especially as I was fool enough to back him for a lot of money last night."

"What made you do that, Cis?" asked the boy.

"Because I was an ass, Harry; because Crymes's sneering manner made me lose my temper. However, I must hope Red Lancer will pull me through. The Cid may not be quite so good as he looks, and as for old Cockatoo, with 10lb. in hand, I fancy I hold him pretty safe."

Stables over, the pair were speedily cantering through the lanes towards the horse-dealer's. By good luck Mr. Mappin was at home, and welcomed the two officers cordially. He was always on good terms, as may be supposed, with the cavalry regiment quartered at York, and in Harry Harperley's case he had known him from a boy, and often lent him a clever pony in the Christmas holidays.

"Come in, gentlemen, and pick a bit. I've a cold round of beef that is not bad to lunch off. Do me the honour to begin with it, and anything I can do for you afterwards, of course I will."

"Well, Mappin, if you will give us some lunch, we shall both be much obliged to you," rejoined Calvert, "and we can talk over what I've come to see you about while we have it."

The horses were put up, and the two quietly seated round the table in the oak-panelled parlour.

"Now, Mappin," said Cis, when he had assuaged a very healthy appetite with the cold beef, and a somewhat unquenchable thirst by a stupendous pull at a pitcher of home-brewed, "I want you to tell me all you know about the horse I bought of you the other day."

"Certainly, Captain Calvert. I picked him up for a song at a sheriff's sale of Dick Hunsley's horses. He was described as 'The Mumper,' a black hunter, aged, and, in that latter particular at all events, correctly, for I should think he's twelve or fourteen years old. I was told he was clever, but, further than he can jump like a deer, I know nothing. I had only had him a week when you took him. To the best of my belief he is what you wanted, a clever hunter, at a low price. I admit freely I turned my money over him. Of course I must, it's my business, but I don't think you paid a pound too much for him."

"You don't understand me, Mappin. Bless you, man! I'm not complaining, I'm quite content with my bargain. But what's the horse's history? that is what I want to get at. Who, for instance, is Dick Hunsley?"

"Dick Hunsley," returned Mr. Mappin, slowly. "Well, about ten years ago Dick Hunsley came by the death of his father into as good a farm as there is in all Yorkshire. The Hunsleys had been yeomen farmers for many generations, farming some two hundred acres of their own, and renting as much more under Sir Tatton, which lay next them. They had always been a straightfor'ard sporting lot, and this Dick was the first of the breed that took to running cunning. It don't pay mostly, and it hasn't with him. He's dead broke, had to sell every acre, every stick, and that's how The Mumper came into my hands."

"What sort of a sale was it?" inquired Calvert. "Had he a large stud?"

"No; they were a very mixed lot," returned the horse-dealer, laughing. "Three fourth-rate racers, a steeple-chase horse, a couple of hunters, and a trapper or two. The Mumper was one of the two hunters."

"Now, tell me this, Mappin. Do you know a man called Isham Boggs about here?"

"I never heard the name in my life, sir," replied the horse-dealer, in no little amazement, "and it is not a name one would be likely to forget either. Might I ask what he is?"

"That is just what I want to ascertain," replied Cis, "and as soon as I do I shall come to you again. And now, Harry, we must be off. Good-bye, Mappin; I've entered The Mumper for our Cup, so anything you can pick up about him I shall be glad to know."

"Entered that old black horse for the

Cup! Well, I'm d—d!" muttered Mr. Mappin, as his guests rode away. "There's an awful fool about somewhere, and who is it? That's the question. Captain Calvert or Robert Mappin? Either I've sold the horse for a third of his value, or else the captain's gone clean off his head."

CHAPTER VI.

AT THE LIGHT HORSEMAN.

"It's odd, deuced odd," said Cis, as they rode slowly back to barracks, "that Mappin should never have heard of this man Boggs. I should have thought Mappin would have known every one who had any connection with horseflesh through all Yorkshire."

"But," interposed young Harperley, "the gentleman with the sweetly euphonious patronymic may not be exactly in that way. Mightn't he be a friend of this Dick Hunsley's, who knows the horse, fancies him, and, thinking he was pretty well given away, is willing to make you a bid for your bargain?"

"I could have understood that if he had gone straight to Mappin, but Mr. Boggs don't suppose Mappin sold the horse to me without turning money over him. He don't even know what I gave for him. It looks to me as if Mr. Boggs was anxious to get back The Mumper at any price."

"Which must mean," exclaimed Harry, "that the old black is a great deal better than either you or Mappin had an idea of. I shall win Strangford's money after all."

"Well," rejoined Cis, laughing, "if The Mumper can get round the course about half as quick as you can arrive at a conclusion, I should say you would; but I've a good deal to learn about that horse, and, amongst other things, whether Red Lancer can't beat him easily."

"I suppose you'll send Murphy to see Isham Boggs?" remarked young Harperley.

"No, I think not. Tim is an excellent servant, but he has a slight weakness, and

I don't consider a gentleman who lives at the Punch Bowl Tavern an eligible friend for him. No, I shall give him strict orders to avoid all acquaintance with Mr. Boggs, and to keep whisky at a distance till after the races; and I tell you what, Harry, you had better say nothing about the mysterious Boggs."

"All right," replied Young Harperley, as they turned into the barracks; "but you'll let me know if you hear any more of that worthy, won't you?"

Cis nodded assent.

Now, there was no one connected with Her Majesty's —th Lancers so interested about the forthcoming races as Mr. Thomas Blundell; the idea of getting horses into condition for something like real business was to the ex-Newmarket stable-man quite exhilarating. He assumed an aspect of profound responsibility, and could not have looked more impressed with the cares of his position had he carried the key of

West Australian's box in his pocket. As a matter of precaution, he knew the form of every horse in the regiment; who could say such knowledge might not some day be useful, and the Major recognize once more that the finality of horses was racing? Still, there was one of which Mr. Blundell considered he had never satisfactorily got the length, and that was Captain Calvert's chestnut horse, Red Lancer. Mr. Blundell was much exercised in his own mind as to how he might induce Tim Murphy to give him just a feeler with old Cockatoo as to Red Lancer's quality.

The proceedings of the mess-room are canvassed in the barrack-room more often than the denizens of the former imagine. Mess waiters, who are perpetually in and out, and whose presence is rarely noticed, are scarce likely to be miracles of discretion. Officers' servants, it stands to reason, must know a good deal of their masters' proceedings, and if master and man are of a sporting turn the chances are that the servitor is as well acquainted with the contents of the betting-book as the compiler. Men of the Crymes stamp may keep such volume under lock and key, but the majority leave it on the table when not likely to require it. There is nothing singular, therefore, in the barrack-room being tolerably well posted in what goes on in the mess-room. Mr. Blundell, prowling about in pursuit of information, is not long before he hears of the entry of the mysterious Mumper, and further, that Captain Calvert has backed his pair against those of the Major for a biggish bet. If the Newmarket ex-stableman is somewhat surprised, he is no whit dismayed, far from it, a racing mystery is to him what chess problems and double acrostics are to some people. It was a veritable duel then between him and Tim Murphy, and Mr. Blundell smacked his thigh and chuckled with delight at the idea of turning the Irishman inside out.

He was quite aware of Tim's amiable weakness; he knew that though he rarely got drunk in a military sense (it took a good deal to do that in those days), he was fond of a glass, and wont to be garrulous when his throat had been sufficiently lubricated. Other people might wonder what on earth could have induced Captain Calvert to enter that old black horse, but this merely aroused Mr. Blundell's suspicions. A regular plant he thought, most likely arranged by Mappin and Captain Calvert; the two horses had been tried together, and 'the ugly duckling' had proved the better of the pair. Calvert immediately takes that, and the next thing is to stick the Major with the good-looking Cid. The grey is sure to be made first favourite for the Cup, as indeed Blundell has learnt he already is, which will enable the Captain and Mappin to back The Mumper for a nice little stake. Such was Mr. Blundell's theory of 'the little game,' as he called it, and it must be borne in mind that, from his stand-point, there was nothing wrong in all this. He didn't see that a piece of sharp practice such as this could be hardly stooped to among brother officers. No, it was smart, very; Captain Calvert had bought the best steeple-chaser Mappin had—all the more valuable because he didn't look it—and was doubtless grinning to think that the Major had bought one he knew he held safe.

Still, although Mr. Blundell, whose belief in his own acuteness was unbounded, made no doubt whatever that he had got to the bottom of things, yet he could not but acknowledge to himself that a little corroboration would be more satisfactory. When you do intend a *coup* it should be made as certain as lies within your power was Mr. Blundell's sentiment on all matters pertaining to the Turf, and he was wont to shake his head in doleful fashion over a certain Derby which had cost him dear some year or two before. The success of one of the Southern competitors had been carefully arranged for, but, alas! the manipulators had not thought it worth their while to trouble themselves about a North country outsider, and the result was discomfiture to the schemers and their friends.

In pursuance of this policy, Mr. Blundell took the readiest opportunity of suggesting an adjournment to the Light Horseman, after their horses were suppered up for the night, to his Hibernian compeer.

"A quiet pipe, just a moistening of our throttles, and perhaps a little palaver over the races. Mr. Murphy, I'd never refuse a hint to a pal myself, that is, one I could trust not to go gabbling about all over the place, and I think it's pretty plain either you or I'll take the Cup."

"Sorra a one of me knows," rejoined Tim. "Ye've a great horse in The Cid, there's no denying, and Old Cockatoo's useful, but I'm thinking Red Lancer 'll throuble yez something."

"All right, then we'll go down to the Light Horseman after we've done with the horses, and have a smoke and a talk over things."

"Faix and I'm agreeable," rejoined Mr. Murphy with a confidential wink. "May be, we might go near settling it to-night."

Tom Blundell was so pleased with the way in which his overtures had been met, that he already regarded the race for the Cup in his own hands; an affair of which the arrangement was to be quite at his disposal. It was such an opportunity as his heart had yearned for of late, the idea of winning money with cogged dice having always a peculiar fascination for some people. Still, Tom Blundell was essentially one of those to whom early information on either the Turf or Stock Exchange generally proves useless. There are men who can never make up their minds as to how to make the best of their opportunities; they are swayed this way and that, they listen to every one's advice, and are guided by none, and finally, when the *coup* comes off, win nothing, but sit down and anathematize their own want of decision. At least, that is what they really should do, but usually they put the result of their own miserable vacillation on the shoulders of a friend, and curse him freely through a far futurity.

The Light Horseman arrogated to itself the title of a snug tavern. It had perhaps been so some half score years ago, when railways were struggling into existence, and the glories of the road, if on the wane, by no means a thing of the past. Although not on the great highway of the North, there was plenty of traffic through Fulford from Nottinghamshire and West Lincolnshire into York that might have then warranted such *status*, but it had unmistakably now degenerated into a public-house depending considerably upon the custom of the cavalry regiment stationed at the northern metropolis. Its situation, about half way between the barracks and the city, gave it an advantage not to be gainsaid, and the military were naturally much considered at the Light Horseman. The landlord understood his customers and their requirements. There was the commodious taproom for the troopers, and the snug parlour at the back of the bar for the non-commissioned officers, to say nothing of a couple of small rooms at the back for gentlemen who had private business to transact. At the back of the house ran a long straggling garden, containing some two or three rather mouldy-looking summer-houses and a superior dry skittle-alley.

In this paradise Mr. Blundell was a man of mark; free of the non-commissioned officers' parlour, and much respected therein as a great racing authority. He was in receipt of very liberal wages from the Major, and probably had more money to spend than any frequenter of the house, and was free with it. That he should rank high in the good graces of the landlord need scarcely be said; consequently, when Mr. Blundell, accompanied by Tim, made his appearance, and demanded a private room and a bowl of whisky punch, he was met with obsequious smiles, and an immediate compliance with his request.

"Fair tipple, Tim, I think," remarked Blundell, as he put a steaming tumbler of the mixture to his lips. "A leetle too much of the sugar, perhaps, but they always overdo the syrup in the provinces."

"It's aisy suction," said Tim, smacking his lips, "and I'm thinking they'd mend it little in London."

"And who said a word about London?" rejoined Mr. Blundell, sharply. "A fig for London! the metropolis of the Turf is Newmarket. I don't believe breakfasts, punch, or pick-me-ups are properly understood anywhere else; and as for training—"

"Ah! well, they've a notion of it up here, the crathurs," interrupted Tim. "May be you've won the Leger with a south-country horse; but, bedad, ye'll admit ould John Scott made a mess of ye this year at Epsom."

"Ground upsets all calculations," muttered Blundell, a little discomfited, "but fill up your pipe, man; there's as good birdseye in that pouch as I can lay my hands on."

For a few seconds the pair smoked and sipped in silence. At last Blundell observed, imbibing confidence with the punch, "I want to be straight with you, Tim; we must put 'em together, but The Cid's our horse, you may depend on it."

"He's a raal beauty, and it isn't likely Cockatoo can give ten pounds to him is what they do be all saying—"

"Pooh! What do you and I care for the general opinion? I want to know what you're thinking," said Blundell meaningly.

"Is it me? Och troth, I'm of the same

opinion meeself. It's beautiful punch—ah well, as you're so pressing, I'll just take another dandy," and Tim pushed his glass to his companion in admonitory fashion.

A savage expletive was smothered on Blundell's lips as he replenished his guest's tumbler. Mr. Murphy was displaying a want of confidence between man and man that was perfectly disgusting, or an amount of ignorance of the world that amounted to imbecility. Which was it? and Tom Blundell after a moment's reflection decided that *punch must show.* "It's a soothing mixture," he remarked, "and warms a man's heart. A queer start of your master, by the way, nominating that old black screw he bought the other day—"

"I'm thinking he's going on the off chance, like the man we saw down at Carmarthen Steeple-Chases."

"Ah, what was that?" inquired Blundell.

"Well, you see, I was down visiting with the Captain in those parts a year or two back, and there was a gintleman who insisted upon putting a clever cob he had into a hunt race; the others all laughed at him, but although there was siven runners he finished second, d'ye see. 'Not quite such a fool as you thought me,' says he, as he weighed in. 'I got five of 'em down, and if I'd got one more I'd have won clever.' The black's a grate lepper, and may be the Captain thinks most of them won't get round."

"I don't fancy that's quite the Captain's view," rejoined Mr. Blundell, eyeing his companion keenly. He could not quite make Tim out; was this pure simplicity, or was it affected stupidity assumed for the purpose of baffling inquiries. But the Irishman's face, though flushed with the punch, baffled all scrutiny as he pushed his tumbler significantly across the table. Blundell promptly replenished the glass, and then resolved to provoke Tim, if possible, to show his hand by depreciation of The Mumper. "I suppose," he continued, "he's made a bad buy of it, that's the fact; and thinks entering the black horse for the Cup will make people believe him better than he is, and so enable him to get out."

"Get out is it," rejoined Tim, upon whom the punch was telling, "it's mighty little throuble he'd have about that. Sure, the masther could turn his money to-morrow av he chose."

"That's easier to say than to do, Master Tim," laughed Blundell. "Some of our officers ain't very wise, but I don't think there's one of 'em fool enough to bid money for The Mumper."

"An' who said one of the gintlemen wanted him? Tho', perhaps, Major Crymes might lay out his money worse, as maybe he'll own when he finds himself at the bottom of a ditch, with The Cid on the top of him. It's a York gentleman who's so sweet. I suppose you've heard of Mr.

Boggs in these parts? He's the boy for sport, whether it's cock-fighting or steeple-chasing. 'What's the Captain want for him?' says he to me the other day.

"'I don't know,' says I.

"'Just tell him to drop me a line,' says he, 'an' I'll take him off his hands at anything in reason.'"

Mr. Murphy was wont to be somewhat braggadocio when he had a little liquor in him.

"Why, what does Mr. Boggs want with him?"

"'Deed I don't know, but from the look of him I'd think it's a team of hearse horses he's collecting."

Once more Mr. Blundell glanced keenly at his guest. Was there any grain of truth in his rodomontade, or was he playing a part? He came to the conclusion that Tim was at all events somewhat under the influence of drink. "And where does Mr. Boggs live?" he asked at length.

"I'm not just at liberty to mention," rejoined the other, with a sly leer. "Such a rale out-and-outer as he is there's no difficulty about coming across."

"It's no object to me," rejoined Blundell, carelessly, as he threw his tobacco-pouch across the table. "We don't trade in hearse horses ourselves."

Tim filled his pipe, and puffed savagely at it for a few moments in silence, and then growled out, "Maybe the hearse horse 'll astonish you before the year's out."

"Can't very much, when you're going to part with it to Mr. Boggs."

"Tear an ages, man! who tould you that? All I said was that he's mad to buy the horse; it isn't likely we'd part with a clipper like The Mumper."

"Do you mean that?" asked Blundell, eagerly.

"I mane that's what Mr. Boggs thinks him," replied Tim, rather taken aback.

"Ah, and he considers him a good horse, has known him before, and that's why he wants to buy him."

"Not at all, it's just funning I was. He's known the crathur a long while, and wants to buy him back bekase he's an ould favourite in the family."

Mr. Blundell experienced a considerable desire to punch his guest's head, but remembering that was the least likely way to get what he desired out of it, and that the experiment might possibly result in that operation being performed upon his own, he refrained.

"Did ye ever smoke a pipe at the Punchbowl?" suddenly inquired Tim.

"No. Where's that?" rejoined Blundell, no little astonished at the abrupt turn in the conversation.

"Troth, I'm tould it's one of the most elegant taverns in the city."

"But that don't tell me where it is?"

"Where is it?" replied Tim—with the

tendency of an uneducated Irishman, to reply to one question by asking another—"It's in Stonegate; but it's getting late. I'm thinking its time we were on the throt."

There was no denying it. Mr. Murphy was subject to military law as regarded his hours, and it was as well he should be on his way back to barracks again. As he settled for the punch Blundell reflected angrily that it was money clean thrown away unless Tim became communicative on the way home. He had brought this blethering Irishman down here and deluged him with punch for the express purpose of turning him inside out, and getting at all there was to tell about Captain Calvert's horses, and he was walking home with a dim consciousness that the Celt had proved too much for the Saxon. Especially did he intend to know Mr. Murphy's real opinion of that old black horse, and he was fain to own that Tim had not let the slightest hint of what he thought on that point escape him. All attempts at conversation on the way back to barracks proved futile. Tim was seized with an unconquerable fit of taciturnity, and responded to his companion's overtures with incoherent grunts and heavy clouds of smoke from his *brûle gueule.* In short, when they bade each other good night, Blundell felt that his hospitality had been obtained on the most fraudulent pretence, and felt as keenly anxious to be quits with Tim in some fashion as his master did with Captain Calvert.

But if not quite so clever as he deemed himself, the pupil of Newmarket had nibbled sufficiently of the fruit of the tree of roguery to be tolerably quick at putting two and two together. Racing men are wont to be rather rapid in their deductions at times, and don't feel it necessary to see the weathercock to tell them which way the wind is blowing. When Mr. Blundell thought over the events of the evening next day he gradually came to the conclusion that there was a pearl or two of useful information in that bushel of chaff to which Tim Murphy had treated him. First, Boggs was a most uncommon name, which it was hardly likely that Tim would have invented; it was probable, he thought, there really was a Boggs, and that, whether or no he wished to buy The Mumper back, he knew the horse's previous history. Secondly, what made him allude to the Punchbowl Tavern? Tom Blundell had never heard of this hostelry before, and he knew he thought pretty well what houses of call were patronized by the regiment from top to bottom; from the Black Swan in Coney-Street, habitually used by the senior officers, to Harker's in Sampson-square, more confined to sporting sub-alterns, and so on through minor houses, till one arrived at the Light Horseman; but he had never heard any one mention the Punchbowl. Puzzling over these things he began gradually to connect them with each other, and slowly arrived at the conclusion that Mr. Boggs was not unlikely to be met with at that mysterious tavern in Stonegate. Once come to this conclusion, Blundell determined to take the earliest opportunity of inquiring for the shadowy Boggs, and ascertaining whether he had a palpable entity.

CHAPTER VII.

ASKHAM BOG.

THE Punchbowl, although unknown to Mr. Blundell, was in those days a tavern very much in his line. What are called sporting houses are now pretty well out of date; at all events it is no longer the fashion for men about town to frequent them, and the Castle, the Rising Sun, &c., are utterly unknown to the golden youth of our time, favourite haunts as they were with their progenitors. The particular pastimes which they nourished and promoted have fallen into desuetude, and the noble science of pugilism in these degenerate days is apt to bring fine and imprisonment to its enthusiastic followers; ratting can hardly be said to meet with encouragement, while cock-fighting is pronounced decidedly unlawful, albeit no more cruel than pigeon-shooting, and infinitely more sporting. Murder on a large scale, under the name of war, or agrarian outrage, under the name of agrarian agitation, seem to be the only two sports of this description recognized in our advanced civilization. However, in '52 the prize ring, although in its decadence, was by no means extinct, nor would the Coop week at Chester have been deemed complete without a little cocking. To know the whereabouts of such amusements men betook themselves to the sporting houses, where they received what was technically termed 'the office,' that is, were told the place of rendezvous, and could then proceed to admire the dogged determination of Portsmouth Jones, the amazing quickness and science of 'the Spider,' or put their money on the famous 'white piles' of the Cholmondeleys in the

Cestrian city. In a sporting county like Yorkshire it followed of course that such things were, and for information concerning such tournaments there was no better place to look in at than the Punchbowl. More than one celebrity of 'Fancy land' was accustomed to make it his head-quarters during the race week, and the then king of the billiard-table, the Great Jonathan himself, who did for billiards what Matthews did for whist, was a well-known frequenter when business or pleasure took him to the northern capital.

After this preamble it may be easily conceived that Blundell found no difficulty whatever in finding his way to the Punchbowl, and his first feeling was one of no little amazement that so congenial a house should not have come to his knowledge before. A crisp October day was just coming to a close when the ex-Newmarket man stepped across the sill of the tavern in Stonegate. Three or four horsey-looking men were absorbing spirits and water in front of the bar, and carrying on a languid and desultory conversation; they took stock of Mr. Blundell in indolent manner, but when he inquired of the presiding goddess whether Mr. Boggs was staying there, Tom suddenly became aware that the conversation had ceased, and that he had become an object of considerable interest to these loungers.

"No, sir, he's not," replied the barmaid. "Who shall I say asked for him?"

"Never mind my name," rejoined Blundell. "He wouldn't know it if he heard it, but I want to see him badly all the same; when is he likely to be here?"

"Can't say, I'm sure," replied the young lady. "Mr. Boggs is very uncertain in his movements. If you left your name and address he'd perhaps make an appointment."

"Ah! thank you, miss, that's what I'll do. I'll just drop him a line here. I s'pose he'd be safe to get it."

"Sure to in the course of a day or two; he's mostly in three or four times a week."

As Blundell—having bade the barmaid good night—issued once more into the street, "Who is he, and what the devil does he want with Isham?" caught his quick ear, and he marvelled greatly who or what this mysterious Boggs might be.

But that was a point upon which he was not destined to be speedily enlightened. He wrote as he said he would do, and was assured, on calling at the Punchbowl, that Mr. Boggs had got his letter, but he received no reply. He had taken kindly to the house, and now often dropped in there of an afternoon, but never could succeed in meeting Boggs. He had got acquainted with some of the *habitués*, and soon discovered that Isham, as they called him, was well-known amongst them, but what his precise calling might be baffled him. If he inquired what he did? he was generally told "sometimes one thing and sometimes another—he's a many irons in the fire has Isham." Did he know anything about horses? "Well he did ought, he's had a mort to do wi 'un," and a general grin pervaded the company, as if much tickled at the suggestion. Equally indefinite was all information as to his whereabouts. "He was a deal about, was Isham, down South to-day, and up away North to-morrow; he's a busy man is Isham."

Weeks slipped by, and it is no secret by this time in the regiment that the derided Mumper has turned out a good deal better horse than either seller or purchaser had ever deemed him. Cis has been on him, and discovered that both Mappin and Tim are right on the one point—the horse is a magnificent fencer, without an idea of refusing. "He tucks his hind legs under him, and throws himself into the next field as if shot from a catapult; if he'll only face water," says Cis, "I've never owned such a jumper before."

Calvert is fortunately possessed of a few common-sense ideas on the subject of training, and therefore orders that The Mumper shall do but very moderate work. He knows that old horses as a rule require much less work than young ones, and that, when you come to a really old horse, he will sometimes do his best thing when in the eyes of many people half-trained. The black, in his opinion, wanted rest, and, acting on this principle, he told Tim to give him plenty of oats and moderate exercise. The horse didn't put on flesh, but that he was improving was evident by the brightness of his eye and coat, and also by his gaining heart. Still there were many who agreed with Blundell that was no sort of preparation for a horse to go three miles across country, and that jump as he might The Mumper could never be dangerous after the first mile, on account of his want of condition.

Cis has never as yet ridden the black

in the hunting-field, but the York and Ainsty are advertised to meet at Askham Bog, 'the very best fox cover in all England,' as the enthusiasts of those parts are wont to proclaim it, and Cis announces his intention of giving The Mumper a turn to Harry Harperley.

"What fun," rejoins that young gentleman. "I do believe Crymes means to ride The Cid. It will be a sort of trial."

"I suppose your sister will be out?"

"Of course, and the governor too; neither he nor Annie ever miss Askham Bog. It's your first season with us, and you don't know what a festival the first meet at Askham Bog is. Why, half York will be there on the Great North road to see us throw off; always a fox, generally a run, and the only place I should think where it is possible for a crowd not to spoil sport."

Cis Calvert's engagement, though suspected, is not as yet a published thing. Annie had told her story to her father, and Julian Harperley had, as is mostly the case, listened to it with no little surprise. A mother would have foreseen it, but to the widower it came as a revelation. The banker was not altogether pleased. It was not that he thought his daughter ought to do better; he was perfectly satisfied with Calvert's position and family; as for ways and means, he could afford to make Annie such an allowance as would enable them to get along comfortably, but the fact was he did not take to Cis exactly. He had liked him to start with, his son, who was in Calvert's troop, was enthusiastic in praise of his captain, regarding him with all that hero-worship a boy of his age is capable of, but Julian Harperley had of late got it into his head that Cis was something of a gambler. The banker was no purist on this point, he was far too much a man of the world and a Yorkshireman to boot to see harm in betting on a horse-race, but when it came to betting pretty well a year's income on the result he was somewhat staggered by it. He had heard Cis's bet at the mess that night of the nominations; his engagement to Annie had of course involved a clear explanation of his means on Calvert's part. So that Julian Harperley was aware that Cis on that occasion had staked his whole private income on the result of the Cup. A man who will bet so recklessly as that may love his wife very dearly, but make life very hard to her all the same. Very pleasant-mannered are those young gentlemen—

"*Whose fathers allow them two hundred a year,*
And who'll lay you a thousand to ten;"

but they are usually viewed askance by the heads of the family, and the banker feared much that Cis Calvert was somewhat in that way.

"You must not think, my darling, that I am opposing your marriage when I tell you that I wish no positive engagement to exist between you for six months. I have told Calvert so, and he admits that I am not very unreasonable. The words spoken of course cannot be recalled, nor do I wish they should be, but I do want you to be quite sure you know each other. The regiment is not likely to be moved yet awhile, and, though when I gave it a son, I little thought it was to rob me of a daughter, yet I shall not complain if only it is for her happiness. What tacit understanding there may be between you I have nothing to say to, but I wish there to be no formal engagement for six months."

"It shall be as you wish, father," replied the girl, smiling. "As I shall see Cis constantly it will not be very hard to keep our secret for six months."

"I am not so sure about that," said the banker. "It's a lynx-eyed neighbourhood, and much given to what Mrs. Charrington would call putting two and two together, though turning two into one would be the more correct expression in such cases."

This delay Julian Harperley thought would give him time to study Calvert's character, to ascertain whether he really was an inveterate gambler or whether he was merely a man who had made a rash bet in the excitement of the moment, for that it must be held regarded as relative to his income, and if he felt, at the expiration of the stipulated time, that his duty to his daughter required him to solemnly counsel her to break with Cis, well then, was it not better that their engagement should not have been formally promulgated.

Such was the state of affairs between Calvert and Miss Aysgarth on that soft November morning, when all York and its neighbourhood were gravitating up the great North road to Askham Bog. There were sporting pedestrians; there were the mere loafing sight-seers; horsey men on foot, apparently breakfasting on ash plants.

Carriages swept by, with delicate ladies swathed in fur and velvet; tax carts, crammed full of blooming rustic maidens, with rosy cheeks, sparkling eyes, and a perpetual giggle on their lips; solemn gigs, occupied by stout comfortable-looking men and their spouses; vehicles that defied nomenclature, that had started as something else near a century ago, and had been modified from time to time to meet the requirements of fashion, all jogged along midst joke and jollity to see the hounds throw off in the crack cover of the York and Ainsty.

The vendors of apples, oranges, and gingerbread had established their stalls, as usual, by the wayside, and were driving a roaring trade, while at the little inn on the opposite side the road to the famous fox cover, it was whispered the finest old crusted gingerbeer was on sale, a drink apparently highly popular and inspiriting, and known to many of the consumers by the presumably local appellation of 'jumping powder.'

That the hunting men should muster in great force was only natural, but besides these were that numerous contingent who take an occasional day; men who borrow or perhaps hire a horse for the occasion, and amongst these were undoubtedly some very rusty-looking customers, none more so perhaps than a bottle-nosed man, in seedy black, but who sat the sorry screw he was riding, nevertheless, like a workman. The oldiers paraded in considerable strength, and there was no little curiosity among the York and Ainsty men to see them perform. The regiment had only arrived in York from Newbridge in April, bringing with it the reputation of being a very hard-riding lot, and though, of course, this was not quite their first appearance, the hunt considered they had not really had an opportunity of taking stock of them as yet. Then the story of the big bet (I am speaking comparatively) had oozed out, and it was known that the Cup was considered to lie between Crymes and Calvert, who again were recognized by the regiment as the two best horsemen they had. Further, it had become known that each would be riding one of his nominations, and, therefore, it may well be conceived that the pair were the subject of no little scrutiny.

Miss Aysgarth, as she rode up to the cover side under her father's escort, had quite a little staff around her. Calvert, Crymes, her brother, and one or two more of the Lancers were all of the party, and that the popular daughter of the popular banker should receive many cordial greetings was matter of course, but, sad to say, upon this occasion I am constrained to admit that The Cid attracted as much attention as Miss Aysgarth. A Yorkshireman has quite as appreciative an eye for a pretty woman as for a good-looking horse, but he is no more exempt from the worship of new gods than his neighbours. Miss

Aysgarth was charming, but then they had never seen The Cid before.

"If that man and that horse can't go, then all I've got to say is looks go for nothing," remarked a veteran sportsman, after a lengthened contemplation of the grey. "We haven't seen much of the Major as yet, but if you chaps mean catching him to-day, you must be off in good time, mark my word."

The Mumper, on the other hand, attracts but little attention; he looks well, but is a plain horse, and never in his best day could have caught the eye like The Cid. The way, too, in which he is ticked with white hairs indicates that he is no chicken, and the general impression is that Calvert is not riding what will represent him in the Cup.

"Ah! Crymes, giving one of your greys an airing, eh?" said Mr. Charrington, as he rode up, and raised his hat to Miss Aysgarth, "a good-looking one, very, but it's a soft colour; yes, soft, sir, d—d soft!"

"Where's Mrs. Charrington; surely she's out?" asked Annie.

"Yes, but we've got a couple of nieces staying with us, so she drove them over to see the fun; however, she's got her horse here, too, so no doubt you will see her in a few minutes."

Muttering something about paying his respects, the Major moved quietly off on The Cid, but he had little thought of philandering at the bridle-rein of the fair mistress of Byculla Grange. He had a new, and, he firmly believed, a very first-class hunter under him, and Horace Crymes vowed two things to himself that day, that he would know what The Cid was like, and that the York and Ainsty should see whether he could ride or no. He stole quietly along the cover on the far side of the road, creeping up the rising ground a little as the hounds drew that way.

"Now, Cis, don't be absurd," said Miss Aysgarth, in a low tone. "Papa will take every care of me, and you know I never really ride to hounds. I won't hear of your missing the first day from Askham Bog on my account. I want to see if The Mumper can really jump as you say. Look at the little knot creeping up the slope, they are old hands, Cis, stealing forward for a start. Go, or I'll hold you the carpet knight I was once rude enough to call you."

Cis bowed low, and then pressing The Mumper into a smart canter, pushed up the cover side in the direction indicated.

"How very much better that black of Calvert's looks when he is going," exclaimed Julian Harperley; "but come, Annie, although we don't aspire to the first flight, it is getting time we also pushed a little forward."

The few preliminary whimpers that for the last three or four minutes had troubled the ear now swelled into a very babble of tongues, and Cis shook up his horse to catch that little knot of horsemen edging rapidly towards the end of the cover, and which he felt intuitively was composed of a cohort of the hard-riding division. He got there just in time to note that the group were well mounted, and looked like going all over, with the exception of a bulbous-nosed man in seedy black, riding a thorough-bred screw, with fore-legs that made one shudder for the owner's neck. Another minute and a cheery 'gone away' calls attention to the fox gallantly breasting the hill-side. The hounds crash out of cover, a faint roar is heard from the road, dimly recalling the tremendous diapason which announces the fall of the flag at Epsom, hats are jammed on, and catching their horses by the head, the little knot are racing up to the first fence, a somewhat hairy blackthorn, with a ditch on the take-off side, the hounds lying slightly to the left. Some of them charge it almost in line, but all are well over, including, no little to Calvert's surprise, the gentleman in seedy black. Cis looks back, and sees they have got a start for what threatens to be 'a cracker'; he is pleased with his position, and more especially is he pleased with the galloping power The Mumper develops. The old black horse is sailing along with the low, sweeping stride of a thorough-bred, little as he looks like one. Crymes, on The Cid, has settled down to his work just in his front, while, odd to say, Cis finds the bottle-nosed man on the cripply weed lying at his quarters. But—

> "If ever they meant it, they meant it to-day,"

as White Melville sings, and racing over the crest of the hill the hounds stream across towards Swann's Whin at a pace that leaves short time for reflection. "Well away," thinks Cis, "with the pick of the York and Ainsty men, and in for a run. I shall know all about The Mumper before this is over, and be able to make a rough guess at what The Cid can do with him. By Jove, what a fencer he is!"

Whether he meant his own horse or the grey matters little—the remark applied equally to both. Making the very best of a capital start, and riding as if he'd no doubts about his second horse turning up, the Major had succeeded in leading the field, and grimly swore to himself never a soul should pass him that day. If he had driven The Cid rather hard at first, he was riding him coolly and steadily enough now, and no one knew better than Cis how bad a man Crymes was to beat at any time, much more when he had a bit the best of his field, as he had at present. For a moment, so well was The Mumper going, the temptation to race up and really have a shy at The Cid was all but irresistible. Then Cis reflected that his horse was by no means fit, that winning the Cup had now become a matter of no little moment to him, both from pride and pecuniary motives. "No," he muttered, "I'll not ride my horse's head off. Second string, indeed! I shouldn't wonder if he turns out first fiddle when I have to determine which is my best."

The pace was severe, and amongst the select few right up with the hounds, the two dragoons occasioned no little curiosity. New-comers with a reputation are always keenly scanned in the hunting-field, and when the pair are supposed to be riding the very horses on which they propose to shortly contest a race, the interest of the lookers-on is, of course, heightened. But there was, perhaps, no one of that select band who watched the relative going of The Cid and The Mumper so closely as the bottle-nosed gentleman in seedy black. How he kept with them at all was a mystery, as neither he nor his horse gave the faintest sign of such capability. A little under a mile and he began to tail; a couple of fields more, and the plucky screw he was riding galloped into a fence completely pumped, and deposited him on his back in the adjoining enclosure. The man picked himself leisurely up, bestowing in the first instance no manner of notice on his luckless steed, but gazing steadfastly after the receding horsemen.

"By G—d," he exclaimed, "the old horse has got back his form, and if these soldiers don't mess him about with too much work, that Cup's as good as on Captain Calvert's table. Poor Dick! I thought his break-up had put an end to the little game we meditated, but it looks as if other people were going to play it for me. I've not quite cyphered it out yet, but it strikes me I shall have a pretty good race over that Cup whatever wins."

And now occurred one of those distressing episodes so familiar to hunting men, when revelling in all the delights of a good start for a good thing. The hounds suddenly threw up their heads, and checked. What was it? Had they overrun it? It gradually became apparent that was just what had happened. The fox had been headed, and, after circling round to the right, had doubled back again to the friendly shelter from whence he came. Maledictions on their luck burst from the lips of the leading division of horsemen. It was disgusting; they were well away, riding delightfully jealous, and in a moment the cup was dashed from their lips. But to one of the cruelly-disappointed band there came balm speedily. A road ran adjacent to the scene of the disaster, and amongst the macadamite contingent that the check had permitted to come up Cis espied a certain riding-habit, which completely changed the current of his thoughts. Leaving the hounds to puzzle out the lost trail, he jumped his horse quietly into the road, and once more took his station by Miss Aysgarth's side.

"I tell you what, Calvert," exclaimed the banker, "they may laugh about the old black at the mess-table, but, by Jove, they'll none of them laugh much at him in the hunting-field. Why, he's a rare galloper as well as jumper. We've managed to keep you in view all the time, and you looked as if you'd take some beating to-day."

"Yes, I think I've picked up a cheap horse," replied Cis, laughing, "and feel that for once in a way I really have had the best of a deal with Mappin."

CHAPTER VIII.

A SUBLIME SACRIFICE.

"Only to think of The Mumper distinguishing himself in that fashion! As Papa said, we could see you capitally all along, and you looked like being right in front all the way to Swann's Whin, which we all thought his destination," said Miss Aysgarth.

"It most probably was, but circumstances at times compel foxes to change their minds as well as human beings."

"A remark pregnant of meaning, no doubt, but I don't see how it particularly applies just now," rejoined the young lady demurely.

"In this way; having been done out of my gallop, I decline to lay myself open to further caprice on the part of the fox family for to-day, and elect to ride with you instead."

"Nonsense! see, they've hit it off again, and you're losing a start."

"Don't be sarcastic, Miss Aysgarth," returned Cis, laughing. "There's not much fun to be got out of muddling back with the pack to Askham Bog."

"But to think of a man dangling by a lady's rein when hounds are running, be it ever so slowly."

"I would willingly forego the best run of the season if I might linger at yours," replied Cis in a low tone.

"You don't really expect me to believe that, do you? Some one has said that 'all females love exaggeration,' but don't you think, Cis dear, you are carrying it just now a little too far, and even if there be a wee bit of truth in it, tell it if you like in Gath, but for the sake of all you hold dear never whisper it in Yorkshire."

"I'd not shrink from proclaiming on the steps of the York Club that a ride with Annie Aysgarth was of better worth than the best run ever galloped from Askham Bog."

"Hush!" exclaimed the girl with a mock affectation of terror. "Cis, dearest, you are talking blasphemy; that exclusive body would cast you out from among them as a barbarian, and taboo me as the Circe who had ensnared Ulysses."

"Well then, we'll revert to the more worldly and cowardly policy, and vow we lost the hounds—must, you know, if we don't follow them?"

"And yet that is what we came out to do."

"In a qualified way. Please remember this ancient but valuable animal I am riding has an important engagement, and I am bound not to ride his head off. I wanted to give him a gallop, but not a hard day."

"Yes, and I am told you have got a terrible lot of money on it, Cis."

"Who told you? your father?"

"No, Harry. I wish you wouldn't bet, at least so high as you did the other night. It will do you harm with papa; he always looks rather askance at men who gamble."

"But, my dearest Annie, I don't. Crymes was speaking in such contemptuous terms of my horses the other night that I lost my temper, and made a foolish bet if you like, but I neither play nor bet as a rule, except in quite a modest way."

"I am afraid, from something papa said, he thinks otherwise. It was that made me question Harry, and so learn all about what took place at the mess. Harry, by the way, is immensely mysterious about The Mumper. He told me he had backed him, that nobody knew what he was, and that you had got some private information concerning him, and then," added the girl, laughing, "he seemed so swelling with irrepressible stable secrets that I maliciously declined to manifest further curiosity."

"Harry is foolish to talk so," replied Cis, smiling, "though, as far as I am concerned, secret he has none to divulge. What the mysteries of his own stable may be I can't say. We're as near the cover here as we want to be, and shall have a good chance to see them go away again, if they manage it."

"No fear but what they will do that," said Miss Aysgarth, "though, perhaps, not with the same fox."

She was right in her prognostications. A few minutes more, and once again re-echoed the many-throated chorus. Again the jealous riders with whom

"While horses can wag it is never say die"

steal forward to the end of the cover. A crash, and the dapple-coated pack pour over the fence like a mill race. A melodious 'gone away' from their scarlet clad chiefs, faintly re-echoed from the Great North road, and the pageant streams along before their eyes, a repetition almost of the first burst.

"By heavens, what a glorious sight!" exclaimed Cis, as his eyes flash, and his cheeks flush; "and look, Annie, there's Crymes away well in front again; ha! the York and Ainsty men must ride to-day if they mean to take down our number. The best man we have leads them just now, and I verily believe on the best horse in the regiment."

"I'll not believe him the best man, nor The Cid the best horse, till a warrior I wot of has gone down before him in the Cup," cried Miss Aysgarth. "If a girl don't have faith in her lover, all creeds are torn up as far as she is concerned; but he can ride, Cis; just look at the way he's pulling his horse together over that awkward little bit of ridge and furrow."

"And if that isn't the way to hand one over post and rails, I never saw it done," cried Cis enthusiastically. "Belief in oneself is a good thing no doubt, but the way Crymes is leading the field to-day is somewhat calculated to shake it."

They were trotting and cantering briskly along the road all this time, with a very fair, though gradually decreasing view of the hounds. Still, as long as they could see them that gallant grey held a commanding lead, which his rider looked resolute to maintain, riding straight as an arrow and indulging his horse with just what came in their way.

"I don't think we shall see much more of them," said Cis at last as he pulled up at the top of a small hill.

"No," said Miss Aysgarth, "they are vanishing fast in the distance, going where you should be going also—to Red House.

It's very sad, Cis, and I quite sympathize with you. Ah, why did you take charge of me instead of wooing fortune once more? You might have cut down Major Crymes, and made a name in Yorkshire story; who knows?"

"I do," replied Cis gaily. "And I'll make that name yet. When I've carried off the prettiest girl in the county, and disposed of Crymes in the Regimental Cup, even the club will admit my conduct to-day as madness with a purpose in it."

"Ah me! yes. 'Young Lochinvar has come out of the West,' but before he carries off his bride in old Border fashion will he permit her to give him some tea? Let's ride home to The Firs, Cis, and have a quiet gossip over the fire. I declare papa has abandoned me in shameful fashion; to leave his loved daughter in charge of a hard-riding dragoon, is equivalent to desertion of the most unpardonable description."

"Nothing of the sort," retorted Calvert, laughing. "It only shows the high estimate he places upon the sagacity and prudence of the horse-soldier. It's only young ladies, as a rule, who properly value the dragoon as a *chaperon.*"

"Poor things," cried Miss Aysgarth, with a burst of merry laughter, "but here's a lovely stretch of turf for a canter, so let's make the most of it."

On arrival at The Firs they handed their horses over to the grooms, made their way to the drawing-room, and Annie rang for tea. Very pretty did the girl look in the brightly-flashing firelight that still gallantly held its own against the fast falling shadows of a November afternoon. She had thrown aside her hat, and the dusky tresses gathered into a knot behind the small, shapely head, and falling low over the broad forehead, glistened like a rook's wing in the flickering light of the flame. The dark blue eyes shone with marvellous softness as they glanced proudly on the man she loved, while the close-fitting habit showed off her lithe, supple figure to perfection. The gay badinage of the hunting-field had ceased, and the conversation carried on between them now was low of tone and earnest of purpose. Cis was mooting his plans for the future, telling her how, for the present, it was incumbent on him to stick to his profession. Would she mind following the steel scabbards about the United Kingdom? There was no chance of their being ordered abroad for years. Some of those Irish quarters were, he knew, deadly dull, certainly, but they had just finished their turn there, and had all England and Scotland before them.

"No, Cis," she gently replied, "I shouldn't like you to give up your profession. I think any woman whose love was worth having would never wish that, as long as her husband had health and strength. A man has his appointed work to do in this world, and it's more likely to be bad for his wife than anybody when he shirks it."

"I am a little afraid that your father will expect it."

"No, Cis, you don't know papa; he's the last man to expect it. No," she added, with a smile, "when he gives me to you it will be with full permission to enroll me in the D troop at once. And now, my own, I must send you away. It's long past five, and I have to clothe myself in splendour preparatory to driving over to dinner at Byculla Grange. Kiss me, Cis, and say good-bye."

He clasped her in his arms, and pressed his lips to the rosy upturned mouth so freely yielded to him, and then, with a whispered God bless you, darling, passed out into the dark November night. Cis Calvert was doomed to think over that day the hounds met at Askham Bog in many a far-away land before Annie stood at the altar with him, and little guessed as he rode gently home to barracks, musing over the roseate prospect before him, what pitiless buffets fate had in store. A run sacrificed, and a horse in training brought home like a common hack in this fashion; verily I think a Yorkshire jury would have found Cis guilty of being close bound to Miss Aysgarth's apron-strings.

There was much talk about Crymes and The Cid amongst the hunting-men as they jogged home after the day's work; both horse and man were honestly lauded, for there was no denying that the Major led the field from Askham Bog to Red House, and never a one could wrest the pride of place from him. Freely they admitted that he had shown himself both 'a customer' and a sportsman, but as far as this last goes, it happened to be just one of those occasions when a master of hounds might have cried gaily, "Now, gentlemen, ride over 'em if you can!" Still, Crymes was the undoubted hero of the day, and those who did not see individually, concurred with those who did, anent Rufforth drain, when, in the words of the late laureate of the hunting-field—

> "They told me that night he went best through the run,
> They told me he hung up a dozen to dry,
> When a brook at the bottom stopped most of their fun,
> But I know that I never went near it—not I."

That there should be much converse about this at Byculla Grange after the ladies left the table was only natural, and that it should be talked about, as it related to the coming steeple-chases of the Lancers, was merely what was to be expected. The rivalry between Crymes and Calvert had already attracted attention to the race for the Cup, and the way the grey has carried him to-day undoubtedly prepossessed men in favour of the Major's chance. Still there were not wanting those who had seen the first burst and recognized what a show Cis had made on the black.

"Calvert went quite as well as Crymes in that first spin, and," added the host, oracularly airing that peculiarly conceived hobby of his, "I've no belief in greys."

"Seeing is believing, Charrington," retorted a bluff hunting squire opposite, as he tossed off a bumper of port. "I don't like your gaudy-coloured ones myself, but I cave to public form when I see it, and if Captain Calvert's got one in his stable better than the one the Major showed us the way with to-day, all as I can say is he's lucky."

"I agree with Charrington. The Mumper went wonderfully well till the check, and I don't think there was much to choose between black and grey that time," said Julian Harperley quietly. "Why Captain Calvert didn't persevere, I can't say."

"Because he knew that old horse of his was about spun out; they do for a spurt, but they can't stay when they are really aged."

"No, I don't quite think that was his reason," rejoined the banker with an amused smile.

And then came much more discussion about the day's sport, and the *pros* and *cons* of black and grey were argued out with much intensity, fortified by that conclusive expression of opinion common to Englishmen, an offer to bet upon it. No little wagering in a mild way was the result of this after-dinner argument, and had it come to a poll there could be no doubt that the greys had it.

The sole representative of the —th Lancers present, as it happened, was young Harperley, and that he should ardently champion his captain, in whom his belief was unbounded, was quite in accordance with the natural hero-worship of boyhood. Chaffed and too closely pressed by those shrewd old sportsmen who surrounded him, what wonder he took refuge in the indefinite, and more than hinted that Cis had knowledge of The Mumper they little dreamed of, and that when the time came they were destined to be considerably astonished by that noble animal's capabilities. "Backed him! of course he had," cried the boy, flushed with excitement. "Had he not taken Strangford's book about him? Only let them wait and see what a mess Calvert would make of Crymes and The Cid when the day came."

If there was a man at that table this talk puzzled it was Julian Harperley. A few weeks back and his son had done nothing but dilate on the certainty this race was for The Cid; that he had turned round and changed his opinion was nothing. Young people often do that, and, alas! there are old ones, too, who when it comes to racing could tell sad stories of what vacillation has brought upon them; but why should Harry so persistently contend that his owner knew The Mumper to be very different from what he was believed to be? Calvert himself always declared he knew little about the horse, and Mappin less.

Was this misty, undefined knowledge he hinted at merely Harry's own particular opinion, and was he indulging freely in that dearly-loved weakness of youth—the backing of it?

I always admire a man who has an opinion; there are so many who have not, whatever they may think to the contrary; specially is this the case about Turf matters. When Jackson confides to me that such a horse will win the Derby, I know that he means such a sporting writer says he will, and when Clackson breathes his views of the political situation into my ear I am also aware that I am receiving an abstract of the leader in the *Standard*, the *Times*, or it may be the *Daily News*. A friend of mine some years ago declared his intention of listening to no advice concerning a certain big race about to be run, but "to play off his own bat" and have at least the satisfaction of losing his money in his own way. Well, he lost his money by a head, and subsequent running showed that he ought to have won it. The result was soothing, if not lucrative. Still satisfied vanity, with pockets well emptied in sustentation of its opinion, is not, upon the whole, a pleasant reminiscence, while, saddest of all, he has held positive and of course expensive opinions ever since—luxuries these to be indulged in only by the rich.

But nobody out had been so much impressed with The Mumper's performance as the hero of the day himself. Crymes had noticed with no little astonishment how well Cis Calvert had gone up to that first check; he had noted that the black was a remarkably fine galloper, as well as jumper, and had seen a great deal too much of racing not to know that they run in all sorts of shapes. He could call to mind, too, some big things done by horses supposed past their prime, and especially in cross-country conflicts had the equine veterans distinguished themselves. He was perfectly well aware, too, why Cis had not persevered, and could not disguise from himself that the Cup was not quite such a certainty as he had booked it, and that his chance of winning Miss Aysgarth looked wofully distant and dim. Difficulties never discouraged Horace Crymes, and though he seldom fell into the error of under estimating an adversary's hand, it never cowed him. He patted The Cid on his neck as they jogged home from Red House, and muttered, "You're dirt cheap at the price I paid for you, and, although that black of Calvert's is a good deal better than I had any idea of, I think, my boy, we shall manage to give a good account of him on the 12th." Then he fell to musing over his chance with the banker's daughter, and was fain to admit that unless something occasioned a breach between Miss Aysgarth and her lover, their engagement would be a thing published to society before many weeks were run. That it already existed he thought probable, but still it was a little in his favour that it was not as yet announced. He held no frivolous scruples about being 'the something' himself, did he only see his way, but at present he most certainly did not. A man of a curious, but by no means uncommon code of morality, Crymes held all fair in love, and a good deal fair in racing, that would hardly seem so to the uninitiated; that bets must be paid while debts were by no means obligatory, and that cheating in love was a thing to jest about, while cheating at cards put a man outside the pale of society. A singular creed, no doubt, but pray do not run away with the idea that it numbers a paucity of believers.

There had been two other lookers-on at Askham Bog that day, who had taken no little interest in the respective performances of The Cid and The Mumper, in the persons of Mr. Robert Blundell and Tim Murphy, and the way Cis had kept his place in the first burst clinched the former's original conclusion that the whole thing was a regular plant arranged between Mappin and Captain Calvert. Strongly imbued with this notion, he determined to once more pump Tim as they rode home together after the hounds had fairly gone away in the direction of Red House.

"Ah, well, the cat's out of the bag to-day, Tim," he observed, "and I don't want to be told you are just exercising the second string as well as myself. Red Lancer looks well," he continued, throwing a critical eye over his companion's horse, "but the Captain will no more want him on the 12th than my master will this old white beggar."

"Oh," rejoined Murphy. "Ye'd have to travel west of Athlone to pick up such a lovely lepper as that ould black. It's a murthering shame the master didn't have another go on him."

"Do you mean he's an Irish horse?" said Blundell, sharply.

"An' couldn't ye tell that by the ways of him?"

"No, nor you either! he jumped well, but so did The Cid, for the matter of that."

"You're a man of mighty little observation," rejoined Tim. "Didn't ye see the crathur wouldn't pass 'a habit.' It's a way they have, though they'll follow them annywhere, an' on mee sowl, the men are much the same when it comes to a petticoat."

"Pooh, what rubbish you talk," returned Blundell, angrily. "I thought, perhaps, your friend Mr. Boggs had told you how that old black is bred."

"My friend Mr. Boggs!" ejaculated Tim, uneasily. "Where did you hear anything about Mr. Boggs?" The Irishman had utterly forgotten his indiscretion that night at the Light Horseman.

Tim Murphy's uneasiness didn't escape Blundell. He leant forward in his saddle for a moment, as if adjusting the throat-lash, and then said, "How did I hear about Isham Boggs? Why at the Punchbowl Tavern in Stonegate, of course, he's always there, you know."

"No, I don't. Why should I?"

"I'm sure I can't say, but I suppose you'll admit you do know Isham Boggs? At least you said so that night we'd a pipe at the Light Horseman."

"Ah, shure! I remember, I've met a gentleman of that name," replied the sorely repentant Tim, now cognisant that his tongue had been running riot.

"And does he not know all about The Mumper, and what a great horse he is?" continued Blundell, marking the effects of his random shot. "Ah, well! my friend don't confide in me, but I fancy you'll find more than one at the Punchbowl who knows the old black besides Isham Boggs."

Mr. Murphy vouchsafed no reply, but producing a short black pipe from his pocket, proceeded to leisurely illumine it, and puff away in moody silence.

"If you won't be sociable, you won't," said Blundell, at length, "and if you won't be confidential, you won't. I should like to have arranged things comfortable with a brother trainer," and the scamp rolled the last words out with unctuous significance, "but if you won't, well, again, you won't. I shall likely know as much about your horse as you before the day, and mind you, Mr. Murphy, we win the Cup, and you don't, if your d—d old hearse horse can take the Shannon in his stride."

"Ye'd be mighty good at brag, an' it might take about two days to skin you in the West; but it's aisy to see why you left Newmarket," remarked Tim, meditatively.

"And why, I should like to know?"

inquired Blundell, in a voice hoarse with restrained anger.

"It's a cruel thing to say of 'em, but I'm thinking their ways were a thrifle too straight for *a trainer* like you."

Mr. Blundell smothered a strong expression, and putting old Cockatoo into a sharp trot, left his unsociable companion without further remark.

CHAPTER IX.

ISHAM THE PROPHET.

In a bedroom on the first floor of the Punchbowl Tavern, overlooking Stonegate, on the evening of the meet at Askham Bog, sat a man, who looked for all the world like a dissolute undertaker. One who habitually drowned the grief of bidding adieu to his fellow mortals in gin, and had gradually come to delight in such 'sweet pain.' He had drawn a small table in front of the fire, relieved himself of a well-splashed pair of antigropolos, and was leisurely consuming a decanter of spirits while he smoked a pipe.

On the table lay pens, ink, and paper, several letters, a *Ruff's Guide*, and a volume or two of the *Racing Calendar*, which latter rather tended to shake belief in the undertaker theory. What Isham Boggs had been originally sometimes puzzled his intimates. A hanger-on of the Turf, and consorting in great measure with that unscrupulous scum to whom racing is no matter of sport but a mere gambling on 'the colour,' he was remarkable, despite his disreputable appearance, for a softness of manner and correctness of speech, which showed that his bringing up had at all events been different to theirs. True when the drink took hold of him, as, sad to say, it too often did, he relapsed into the coarse language of his habitual companions, but otherwise he was

> "The mildest-mannered man
> That ever scuttled ship or cut a throat;
> With such true breeding of a gentleman,
> You never could divine his real thought;"

and if he didn't go quite that length he certainly indirectly made little scruple of slitting purses.

What was his business? Ah, what is the business of some of these turf parasites? I presume it might be designated as raging around and seeking whom they may devour, and a very poor living many of them seem to make of it, but Boggs was not of these. He had a business, and a very extensive business he might have made of it, but in consequence of that miserable failing no one could trust him. Was not one of the mightiest turf *coups* ever planned lost in this wise? There are magnates of the ring yet, I trow, who shake their heads over Blair Athol's year, and muse how wine will steal away the brains of men.

Mr. Boggs was a prophet, not of the sort that concern themselves about either the weather or the end of the world, but a genuine veiled prophet of Khorassan, who had visions of the finish of the Derby, and other important Turf contests. He had barked his opinion as 'Tom Todger's Terrier' in one paper, he had squeaked it as 'the Rat in the Cornbin' in another; but, alack! there were times when editors could get no opinion from either 'Rat' or 'Terrier,' and on non-fulfilment of contract editors are relentless. He was a good judge of racing, and perhaps had somewhat better luck than his brethren in the trade; but a prophet who won't prophesy can no more get a living than a cobbler who will not stick to his last. The oracles of Delphi, I take it, were always on sale, but we should hardly pay for such shadowy prophecy in these times, and the Turf vaticinator who gave the winner of the City and Suburban in a double acrostic would find trade slacken.

The prophetical business having somewhat fallen off after the manner of all neglected industries, and Isham Boggs's passion for strong waters having in like *ratio* improved by cultivation, it behoved that worthy to supplement his original trade by the addition of divers smaller callings, and he became Turf adviser for a consideration to various callow fledglings from the universities, in the army, &c. From that out, the decadence was rapid, and he was soon known as a clever man, who might be bought for the perpetration of any Turf iniquity. It was true that little matter of the wine cup still made against him, but he had a marvellous shrewd head, no scruples, and never babbled in his drink. He had by this time acquired a most undesirable notoriety, and, with the modesty of all great men, was reticent about obtruding either his name or his personality on those likely to recognize it. The fellow, indeed, had more than one alias, but, whatever they might do elsewhere, these stood him in little stead at Newmarket, where he was as well known as the Bushes, call himself what he might. At York it was different; although Isham Boggs was as sure to appear wherever there was horse-racing of sufficient magnitude, still he was more especially a fungus of south country growth, and a man like Mappin, whose race-going was limited to his own and the adjoining counties, was little likely to know anything about the redoubtable Isham.

"Ah!" he said, after a gulp from the tumbler at his elbow, "that spin to-day told me a lot. I wonder whether Captain Calvert had an idea he was in some measure riding a trial; how astonished he'd have been to know that the old cripple racing alongside him would about sweep the board if hurdle-races were run one mile instead of two. Yes," he muttered, meditatively, "The Coiner would take a deal of doing even yet over four flights at that distance; pity the beggar can't stay. Well, I've seen for myself, and my verdict is this—that the old black has come back to his old form, and, if he only keeps right, will win that race on the 12th of next month. If he's beat it'll be by that grey of the Major's. Good horse that, and good man, too, his owner;

from all I hear, there's nothing else in it. Now, how am I to make a good thing of this? I must stand to win on both, and without risk. Oh dear no," he continued, smiling, as he took his pipe from his mouth, and addressed an imaginary audience. "What! lay odds on two! Fie, gentlemen! Poor patient sportsmen like me don't dash it down in that fashion. Our poor brains must serve us in lieu of your well-stuffed money-bags. I don't think it will be difficult for *me* to stand a pretty little stake, for a man in my humble sphere, on both The Cid and The Mumper.

Once more did Isham take counsel of his tumbler, and then proceed to smoke and stare into the fire with steady persistency. At last, knocking the ashes out of his pipe, he kicked the coals together with his boot, and, turning to the writing-table, drew a small note-book from his breast pocket, and said, "Now to look out the man I want. Ha! here we have 'em, bookmakers. I wonder what a publisher would give for this little volume? it would sell. 'A Book about Bookmakers,' how they began, broke, and were buried. Lord! the public would go wild about it. Fancy the biographies of B. Green and Davis; what's fiction compared to facts like that? and I could write it, I could. No," he muttered sadly, as his eye fell on the waning spirit decanter; "no, not now, I could have done, once. Ah, well, now to find the man I want. He should be a north countryman, or he may hardly think it good enough to come so far for, and then—yes, he must be one who doesn't know me too well. Nottingham, yes, there's plenty of good men there, but there's some I don't fancy, and there's some would hardly fancy me. Hah! here is the very man, Bilton of Leeds, new at it, only got into Tattersall's last year, and a dashing bettor. That settles it," and swinging his chair round to the table, Isham proceeded to write a couple of letters, one to the Leeds bookmaker, and the other was subscribed to Mr. Thomas Blundell, —th Lancers, Cavalry Barracks, Escrick Road, having accomplished which feat Boggs finished the gin, and went to bed.

Tom was not a little surprised and elated when he in due course received Isham's letter. The mystery that surrounded the man, the dark hints dropped by the frequenters of the Punchbowl concerning his business, and, above all, Isham's apparently supreme indifference about an interview with Mr. Blundell, had all impressed the ex-Newmarket man with a respect for the unknown Boggs difficult to imagine. The veneration for the unknown is a singular weakness of humanity. Heaven knows what the inhabitants of India thought John Company Bahadoor might be, but he was to them a magnificent myth, such as the Empress of India can never hope to become, and their veneration was in proportion. Japan the same; as soon as that mysterious sham, the Mikado, was exposed to the view of the multitude he perished. What respect can there be left for general officers in an age when they are as many as the sands of the sea shore? The democratic wave of the day is quite possibly due to the excessive plenty of princes of the blood, for humanity in its foolishness is apt to hold cheap what becomes plentiful, and alack! the royalties recall the bygone ballad,

> "We very much winces, at this long list of princes,
> Which is longer than it ought for to be."

The eagles of the earth, like the eagles of the air, should be restricted by nature as to progeny.

Mr. Blundell lost little time in responding in person to Isham's summons. He was conscious of being under the protection of the redoubted Boggs the minute he crossed the Punchbowl's threshold. "Oh, yes, sir," exclaimed the barmaid with a smile, "Mr. Boggs is at home. Here, Sam, show the gentleman up to Mr. Boggs's room," which Sam—called by courtesy a waiter, but with an unmistakable look of potboy about him—proceeded to do.

The great Isham, in all the easy *deshabille* of shirt-sleeves, was busily engaged in writing letters when they entered.

"Sit down, please, Mr. Blundell, and excuse me for one moment. We'll have our talk as soon as I've finished this note."

Tom sat down, and very naturally fell to studying the queer figure seated at the table. A spare man, of medium stature, with a tallowy sickly face, in the midst of which a bulbous nose glowed like the red light above the door of a chemist, close-cut grizzled hair, and clean-shaven cheeks made his age very difficult to define; he might have been anything between forty and fifty-five. He was habited, as far as he was habited, in the sable garments he usually affected, and his linen, as Tim Murphy had observed, was not suggestive of extravagance in the laundry line. But the thing that puzzled Blundell most was a hazy idea that he had somehow seen this man before, though when and under what circumstances he couldn't for the life of him recollect.

"There, that's finished," said Boggs, as he closed his letter. "I am a busy man, Mr. Blundell, and that must be my excuse for receiving you so coolly. It's a poor profession is mine. Great responsibility, and very inadequately remunerated; turf adviser to a lot of young gentlemen who don't know what to do with information when they get it, who back long shots with most injudicious freedom, and take two to one about pretty near a certainty in tenners, bah!" and, disgusted with the picture he had conjured up, Isham threw himself back in his chair and paused.

It is odd, but it is a curious proof of the fascination of the Turf, that belief in these seers of the race-course is never one wit impaired by the exceeding shabbiness of their apparel.

"Who drives fat oxen should himself be fat,"

but that the man who confides Pactolian secrets should himself be wealthy has never been in the least regarded as essential. Why they don't commence with making their own fortune never seems to occur to their credulous clients, and it is curious to notice that the march of education and science never makes the faintest change in human nature. The alchemists of old were, as a rule, badly clad and impecunious, although on the verge of the golden secret, but never wanted patrons; and that many a noble Athenian fell a victim to the confidence trick I have little doubt.

"Now some of my patrons, Mr. Blundell, will be coming over to these races of yours," resumed Isham, "and, of course, they'll want my advice about what they are to do. I don't mind paying a trifle for information, and I should think if any one does know what'll take the Cup it's the trainer of The Cid."

"What might you call paying for information?" inquired Tom sulkily, this not being at all what he had expected from the interview. He had dreamed of an elaborate fraud, and Isham's proposition was a mere picking of pockets.

"Oh! I'm generally pretty liberal," replied Boggs carelessly. "It pays best. It's a small race this, you know, not much to be made out of it. I should think a fiver ought to satisfy you."

"So you sent for me to make me such a bid as that, did you?" said Blundell, rising in great dudgeon. "You manage your affairs, and I'll manage mine, we don't row in the same boat. I can't put a name to you yet, but I've seen you before, I'll take my oath."

"Stop, stop, my good fellow," cried Isham; "nonsense, we don't part like this. You'll wet your whistle, and we'll talk things over quietly. Sit down, man. You must be pretty green at the game if you fancied I was going to trust you right off."

"You'll have to do it sooner or later if you and I are to do business," replied Blundell sullenly, as he resumed his seat. "You don't suppose a man as was raised at Newmarket is going to make only a fiver out of a chance like this."

"Ah, you were brought up at Newmarket, were you?" rejoined Isham, and his light blue eyes surveyed his visitor in the keen, stealthy, half absent manner a cat affects when playing with a mouse. "They rather neglected your education I'm afraid, or you ought to know your master's neither a fool nor a man to play tricks with. Has the name of being liberal, too," continued Boggs dreamily, as if talking to himself; "upon my word I shouldn't wonder if I made a better thing of it by playing on the square."

"Confound it! what do you mean?" exclaimed Blundell.

"Only this—the Major knows me, and

if it came to his ears that you had been calling upon me I don't think you'd have much more to do with The Cid or any other horse of his."

"I don't know who you are, and I don't care," retorted Blundell, roughly. "What I came here for anybody's welcome to know. I came to find out all I could about The Mumper. I was told you knew the horse, and wanted to buy him back again from Captain Calvert."

"I look like buying horses, don't I?" said the other, with a derisive glance at his habiliments.

"You might be buying for other people. I wanted to know what chance that black horse really had in the race."

"That depends upon me," rejoined Isham Boggs quietly. "The Cid's chance depends upon me also, and I haven't quite made up my mind as to which I'll win with."

Tom Blundell's face was a study. "Why,

damme," he said, "you don't mean to say that you have anything to say to our horse?"

"And this to a man," observed Mr. Boggs, addressing once more an imaginary audience, "who has had twenty-two Derby runners in his pocket out of twenty-four. It would be always rash, my friend, to say that I'd nothing to say to any horse in any race in which I took an interest. With regard to your horse, his winning depends a good deal upon how I think it will suit me. You needn't look so particularly astonished; if you ever *have* been at Newmarket you ought to know that it isn't always the owners who pull the strings; there are occasions upon which they have to take orders instead of give them."

"I know that well enough," rejoined Blundell, "but my master's not one of that sort; nor is a regimental race one worth a money-lender's interference if he was."

"Ah!" rejoined Isham, "what refreshing

innocence. If, as I said before, you ever *were* at Newmarket, it is very transparent why you are not there now. Might I be permitted to observe," and the soft, polished speech contrasted strangely with the man's shabby appearance, "that neither you nor any one else in the regiment know much about Major Crymes; further, that anything money can be made over is deemed worth interference with by some people. Me, for instance."

"All right, I've no doubt you're devilish clever, but I HAVE been at Newmarket, although you mayn't think so," exclaimed Blundell, no little nettled at the contemptuous way in which Mr. Boggs was treating him. "I don't know what the blank and blank you sent for me for; but we'll win that race whether it suits you or not," and so saying, the angry Blundell rose preparatory to departing in his wrath.

"My dear sir, that is just it. No, you decidedly wouldn't do for Newmarket—a little too short in the temper, my friend. Sit down, sit down. You have just told me gratuitously what I offered you five pounds for a quarter of an hour ago; what I sent for you to ascertain."

Mr. Blundell dropped back in his chair dumbfoundered. Who on earth was Isham Boggs? Was he a bookmaker from those torrid climes unnameable to ears polite, and where, oh, where had he seen him before?

"I wanted to know whether you thought The Cid good enough to win, and you do. Now, I've another question to put to you. How do you propose to turn money over this? By backing The Cid, I presume, from what you said."

"I don't know. You carry too many guns for me, and that's a fact," rejoined Blundell. "I'd like to talk the thing over with you quietly."

"Now you're becoming sensible. Listen! I suppose I may assume that there are only three horses in the race, Captain Calvert's two and The Cid; neither that brown horse Mr. Harperley has just bought, nor that Herodia of Mr. Strangford's are any good, eh?"

"I should think not."

"Very well, The Mumper will turn out the best of Captain Calvert's pair, and, therefore, the race, bar accidents, lies between him and The Cid. Now, Blundell, my man, I have about thought this thing out, and you can't pay too much attention to the grey. It will be a very fair certainty for him. All you've got to do is to pitch him out right, and put your very shirt on it."

"That's all very fine," rejoined the other; "but, in the first place, there'll be a very limited market, and, in the second, The Cid will be a strong favourite."

"Very sensibly put," said Isham. "How a young man of your understanding should ever lose his temper and talk nonsense beats me. But these are little points I'm rather happy in arranging; there will be plenty of professional betting, never fear. I'll ensure a ring, and, what's more, your horse won't start favourite."

"It's all very well," rejoined Blundell, "but I don't know whether to believe in you or not. Neither I nor any one of my acquaintance knows anything about Isham Boggs."

"It's a pity the world generally, and especially that portion of it that's addicted to horse-racing, is not in similar ignorance. Though only a travelling name, it would conduce both to my profit and comfort if it were less known. If you have been at Newmarket, you may have heard of Miles Lane, and if you've ever been racing much, he may have been pointed out to you, although he is warned off the Heath."

"Miles Lane!" exclaimed Blundell, starting from his chair. "What, him as was one of the famous Running Rein lot? By Heavens! I thought I'd seen your face before. I remember you was pointed out to me some years ago at Ascot," and Mr. Blundell stared at the magnificent spoiler as if he'd been the prime minister of a Liberal administration of these times.

Isham's vanity was touched. He was not insensible to this spontaneous tribute to his misdirected talents, and, like many of his class, he had ability far above the average—ability that would have raised him a handsome income properly applied, but which as it was appeared to profit him little.

"Yes," he said, "I was in that plant, and it took us a deal of trouble to bring off, too; while, as Goody Levi said afterwards, 'What's the use of winning the Derby when they won't give it you.' Can't you trust me now to manage a little matter like this?"

"Ah, that was just what it was," thought Mr. Blundell; "could he trust Isham? As for his capacity for mapping out any conceivable turf villainy, of that Tom had no doubt; he had heard so many stories of

Miles Lane's audacious frauds in his Newmarket days that he regarded him as a species of race-course Rob Roy, as a man who, if in some danger of the gibbet or the prison from the Jockey Club and that section of society, was the pet hero of the free lances. But then, would the great freebooter act fairly by him ?"

Isham's keen blue eyes read his face like a book, and solved the question for him.

"What, you're not quite sure I'm going no the square with you. Very well ? Now, just pay attention to me. After getting your opinion about The Cid's chance, I might as well have let you go as not. Why didn't I ? Because when I square a race, and I've squared a good many in my time, I always like to have the trainer in the swim. Now, if I let a trainer know I have backed his horse, and that he is on at a comfortable price in a small way, and that he needn't be afraid of such and such horses, he understands they are out of his way. He's a fool if he asks questions; he'd much better not know, and I need scarcely add that things of this sort can't be too little talked about. What's my object then in letting the trainer know? Simply this —if anything goes wrong with his horse, I expect him to let me know at once, that's all. Then we arrange the puzzle again for the public. Now, do you understand?"

"I think so; The Cid is to win, but if anything goes wrong with him, I'm to let you have a line here at once."

"Just so, and in the mean time you are on at 100 to nothing about your own horse. If anything goes wrong with him you'll know what we'll go for—be it The Mumper or anything else. I mayn't look like money, Blundell, and I haven't it, but those who employ me have, and never fail to discharge any obligations of this kind."

He spoke no more than the truth, and it was the wide-spread knowledge of this that made him so dangerous on the Turf.

There was always plenty of unscrupulous men ready to find money to carry out the schemes his subtle brain had wove.

Keep money himself he could not; the moment the necessary restraint for its acquirement was abandoned, the man became a drunken gambler.

Mr. Blundell walked home from the Punchbowl in a state of high moral ecstacy. The Cid was to win the Cup, and he had made the acquaintance of the famous Miles Lane, one of the chief manipulators of the great Running Rein fraud.

CHAPTER X.

THE RACE.

THE excitement about the race for the Cup had not only risen to flood tide in the regiment, but had gradually simmered up into a very respectable boil in the neighbourhood. A local match in the sporting north-country can put the inhabitants into a ferment quiet citizens of the south little dream of; and, by common consent, this race had come to be regarded in that light. It was true, Strangford avowed his intention of coming on Herodia to look after his money, as he said, but nobody had any belief in his chance, any more than they had in young Radcliffe's and two or three more, who declared their intention of having 'a ride' anyway. Neither Crymes nor Calvert made the slightest disguise about which of their respective pairs was the best, and, as Julian Harperley laughingly told his daughter one night, "The Cid and The Mumper were as much in men's mouths round York just now as The Dutchman and Voltigeur had been in the spring of the previous year. Both horses had been out with the hounds upon more than one occasion since the famous day at Askham Bog, but their owners rode them somewhat tenderly, as, with a big race before them, it was only natural they should. Still there was no denying that the Major made much freer use of The Cid than Cis ever ventured to do of The Mumper. This occasioned much adverse comment concerning the black; it was the opinion of many that Captain Calvert's horse could not stay, and that he had a dreadful suspicion of the fact himself; others again opined that he was to some extent infirm, and, consequently, required humouring, while the thorough-going partisans of The Cid pronounced The Mumper a crippled miler, and wondered how any people could be such fools as to back a horse just because he could jump, when he was required to gallop three miles or so besides. It was undeniable that the weight of popular opinion was decidedly against The Mumper, not only in the regiment, but still more so amongst the members of the hunt. Still there was a small but staunch division who believed in that veteran black horse with unswerving fidelity. In the regiment the men of his troop, swayed by that devotion to their Captain which in days lang syne characterized the army, and also by the sanguine prognostications of Tim Murphy, were 'on' to a man. Young Harperley and a small knot of Calvert's intimates stuck stoutly to The Mumper, while the banker, from what he had seen of the horse's qualities that day at Askham Bog, and strengthened further in his opinion by Cis's confidence regarding him, had also got a modest wager on the black and crimson sleeves, while as for his daughter, she was standing those colours for a bale or so of gloves, and immeasurable quantities of sweet anxiety for her lover's triumph.

But, on the other hand, Mappin made no secret of his opinion that there was never a horse in the —th Lancers could make The Cid gallop, that he had no belief whatever in any concealed virtues in The Mumper, that the horse was a useful old screw, especially serviceable up in the cramped Ainsty country, but to talk of him as a steeple-chaser was simply ridiculous. Crymes also expressed, for him, remarkable confidence in The Cid generally, replying to direct questions by the bland rejoinder, "I don't know, but I certainly don't see what's to beat him."

At Byculla Grange also raged contention

and diversity of opinion, for while the mistress of the establishment pinned her faith, and gallantly staked her money to boot, on Major Crymes's white jacket and violet sleeves, her spouse anathematized grey horses, and kept persistently piling a little more on the black, in accordance with the natural contrariness of his nature.

"Yes, madam," he observed viciously one morning in conclusion to some slight argument with his wife as to the probable result of the forthcoming race, "you will be probably broke in purse and Crymes in neck, and, upon my soul, I can't pity either of you," and with a low rumbling about fools putting their faith in grey horses, &c., Mr. Charrington gradually rumbled himself into the stable-yard.

It is the evening before the race, and Harry Harperley, avid of information, and restless as young ones are wont to be before the first big event which befalls their lives, has hied him into York, and dropped into Harker's Hotel to see if there is anything going on. We all know the old joke about "Paris for fashion, London for wealth, but gie me Peebles for plaisure," and so it was in the capital of the north, the Black Swan in Coney-street for swells, Harker's for sport, and the Punchbowl for devilry. Very busy is Harker's that night, for Mr. Bilton, the big bookmaker from Leeds, and many other sporting men have arrived there for the morrow's races, and discussion concerning them waxes high. Very obstinate and cantankerous is that great betting magnate, Mr. Bilton, showing an animosity to greys that would have warmed the heart of the peppery owner of Byculla Grange. Whether it was too much port, or whether the salmon had not suited him, who shall say? but his ominous six to four against The Cid gradually extended to five to two, and when Harperley entered the smoking-room he had just proffered three hundred to one hundred against the

Major's horse. York, as a rule, believes little in a bookmaker being influenced in his business by either irritability or indigestion, and the whisper went about, "What has happened to the Major's horse?" Bookmakers in those days, as bookmakers do in the present, followed the bell-wether like so many sheep, and the smaller fry were as anxious to lay against The Cid as if they had already attended his funeral; they knew nothing, but they assumed Bilton did, and that was quite sufficient reason for following suit.

There were two or three men present, who looked like small tradesmen, who every now and again dribbled a little on The Mumper, and *les ames damnées*, the backers who for the most part are just as sheep-like as their adversaries, the fielders, began to nibble freely in that direction. So much did the furore concerning the black increase, that before Young Harperley left the room he saw Cis Calvert's horse established a strong first favourite at 7 to 4, while 4 to 1 was freely offered against The Cid. Very elate was the Cornet, as after riding back to barracks with the intelligence, he burst into the ante-room and published it. Thereon the followers of the Major were dumbfoundered, while those of Calvert were proportionately elated. As for the principals, neither of them happened to be present, so the gathering men left to muse over the mutability of the equine stock exchange with what equanimity they might.

There was a gathering that night in the bar parlour of the Punchbowl, and from time to time dropped in divers sporting spirits, who having previously peeped in at Harker's, brought the news that there was something apparently wrong with The Cid, as they were laying against him "terrible free in Sampson-square," and pasting the money down on that old black horse of Captain Calvert's, which Mappin, it was well known, had said was of no use whatever. A small knot of men, of whom Tom Blundell was one, exchanged meaning glances on receipt of this intelligence, recognizing, as they did, the master hand of Isham Boggs in the manipulation of the betting market. That mysterious potentate was not present himself. He rarely was on such occasions, and deprecated nothing so much as the dubious celebrity of a public character. He had had fame thrust upon him on one or two occasions, and held it undesirable and inconvenient. There are walks in life in which it is against one's interest to be readily recognized of the public, as in the case of the detective policeman, the burglar, the inquiring philanthropist, &c. Photography in those days was barely in existence, or there would have been nobody to inveigh louder than Isham against the preposterous vanity that prompted display of one's likeness in shop windows. He was given to do, if not exactly good, still whatever he did do by stealth, and quite content to trust that, like virtue, it should bring its own reward, only I am afraid that the incorrigible Isham would have expressed infinite belief in his doings being more profitable than virtue, while it was not probable that any moralist would confound the two.

If ever there was an adorer of Sheitan it was Thomas Blundell. The sect of the devil-worshippers is by no means confined to Asia, but has numberless ramifications in more civilized countries. Blundell's admiration for a clever scoundrel was always great, but for a successful leg it was unbounded. He regarded Isham as other men might a great statesman, a celebrated poet, or a distinguished soldier; he had reverenced the unknown Miles Lane, reputed to have been concerned with every extensive Turf robbery for the last twenty years, but his veneration for this personage since he had met him in the flesh as Isham Boggs was unlimited. The great Boggs having vouchsafed to take this little affair in hand, and decreed that The Cid was to win, why, of course, he would win. Of that Blundell entertained no doubt, and it was in the most jubilant frame of mind regarding the morrow that he walked home from the Punchbowl.

A soft grey December morning heralded the day fixed for the decision of the momentous question as to whether The Cid or Cis Calvert's black were the better animal. Society around York peeped from its windows with no little anxiety as it clad itself in shining raiment, for only let the weather be fine, and the races were bound to be great fun. The Lancers had been profuse in the matter of invitations to lunch, and society had due warrant for supposing itself in for a pleasant outing. Many a fair girl robed herself in fur and velvet that misty morning, in great trepidation as to what the skies might have in store; but perhaps no maiden of them all felt so nervous as Annie Aysgarth. It was a good deal more than spoilt silks or lost gloves to her this tournament, little as she dreamed what it was to be in reality; but she knew Cis had rash and heavy bets upon it, which he could badly afford to lose, and that was enough to make her nervous, let alone the thought that gruesome falls sometimes betide those who ride steeple-chases. She had not been able to conceal her fears from Cis himself only the night before, and he had made light of her anxiety.

"Nonsense, sweet," he laughed, "I know how to fall, never fear about that, and I really do think I shall beat Crymes. Harry and I tried The Mumper and Red Lancer on the Knavesmire the other morning, and over two miles Harry on the black gave me 10lbs. and a handsome beating."

"It is very foolish of me I know, Cis dear; but I shall be wretched till you are safe past the winning-post. In front, I hope, but I confess it will be a relief to me when it's all over."

"You're a foolish young woman," rejoined her lover, as he kissed her; "but mind you've bays with which to crown the victor's manly brow when he returns to your side in the first flush of his triumph; and yes, Annie darling, a beaker of something cooling to assuage his manly thirst. Don't look shocked, there was a deal of thirst about the Homeric period."

"You need not fear my looking shocked; you will be welcomed with jubilant smiles, believe me."

Still, in spite of all this reassuring love talk, Miss Aysgarth felt unaccountably nervous as she stepped into the mail phaeton which was to convey herself and her father to Crockey Hill that 12th of December.

There was a gallant array on the hill when they arrived. A temporary Stand had been erected, and was crowded with the officers and their friends. A large marquee had been pitched at the back, and consecrated to unlimited refreshment, while right and left of the Stand were numerous carriages, tapering off to tax-carts and more humble vehicles, as they receded from that vantage point. In front of the Stand a regular ring had been fenced in, and it was evident that no inconsiderable amount of business was being transacted therein. Mr. Bilton was, of course, the leading spirit, but there were plenty of his *confrères* who conducted business on a smaller scale, the majority of whom were of that class known by the designation of bagmen. 'The Vase,' open to the gentlemen of the York and Ainsty, had been run, and produced a capital race, resulting in the triumph of an outsider by half a length; and now the event of the day stood next on the programme. The bookmakers were having a busy time of it, for the Tykes seemed bent on having a bet of some sort on the Cup.

Sheer weight of money had brought The Cid once more to the fore in the betting, and he had recovered the position he had lost on the preceding evening in a great measure.

Most of the hunting men and the farmers were backing him, his owner and the majority of the regiment were standing by him, and yet Bilton never tired of laying, and his brethren of the mystic circle followed suit. The Mumper still ruled first favourite, although he had but a small following in comparison with The Cid, and could boast of being little more than half a point before his great rival in the quotations. It was curious to note that he was backed chiefly by the York people and strangers in contradistinction to the country gentlemen and farmers, who, with a few exceptions, went for the Major's horse. Of the other three runners, for the field had dwindled down to five, Mr. Strangford's Herodia was fancied by a few who had seen him go well on her in the hunting-field, and Radcliffe had a few believers in him, who entrusted Gil Blas with their investments for the like reason, but Captain Calvert's Red Lancer, ridden by young Harperley, was friendless. People rarely do back the second string of a stable, and yet it is curious how often the crack succumbs to it. Did not the first favourite for the Derby in the present year canter away from his stable companion at Ascot last, while the owner and his friends only awoke to his excellence after losing their money on the other?

Some little way from the Stand, but still quietly edged into an excellent position amongst vehicles of much more pretension, was a York fly. Seated in it, engaged in earnest conversation, were Isham Boggs and Tom Blundell.

"And your horse, you say, is as well as can be wished?" said the former worthy, sharply.

"The Cid is as fit as I know how to make one. In my judgment, Mr. Boggs, he don't want another hour's preparation. He ought to win right out on his own merits unless The Mumper is a deal bigger horse than I think he is."

"Very good. You must be off now. Your master will be wanting you. Listen to me. Mind you come back here the minute the Major has mounted, and wait for me. There will be fifty pounds into your hand when we next meet; but mind I do find you here, because it's just possible your horse mayn't win if I don't."

"Why, what on earth can I have to do with it?"

"Good heavens, man! is this any time to ask questions?" exclaimed Isham, impatiently. "Your master may be inquiring for you this minute. Go, but don't forget what I have told you."

Tom Blundell said no more, but darted off to where his subordinate was leading The Cid quietly about, imbued with more veneration for Isham Boggs than ever.

The excitement is rising in the Stand, wherein most of the heroes of the coming fray are now congregated, their gay silken jackets concealed by overcoats.

What devil prompted Horace Crymes it is impossible to say, but he was suddenly impelled to crave Miss Aysgarth's blessing on his cause, knowing though he did that it could be hardly hoped for. "Won't you wish me good luck?" he said, softly, to the banker's daughter. "I think I should about win if I only carried your good wishes."

"I am sorry, Major Crymes, but both my bets and my sympathies are elsewhere. You can't expect me, you know," she continued, laughing, "to so utterly ignore my own interests as to wish the success of The Cid."

"No," he said, with a mocking smile, "but I also have interests to protect, Miss Aysgarth. I number a large following here to-day, and I am bad to beat when in earnest. I was never more so than I am now; the result of this race seems somehow to symbolize the result of something else that I have set my heart on, and I can give you no better advice than to hedge. The black and crimson will go down before the white and violet, believe me."

He turned away quickly, before she could answer him, and was making his way out of the Stand, when he was arrested by Mrs. Charrington's voice.

"One moment, Major Crymes, before you go. I must wish you all luck in the tournay; remember I have pinned my faith on your colours, and, should The Cid fail me, am a ruined woman. Good luck attend you, Horace," she added, in a lower tone, "and don't be rash, if only for my sake."

Both women looked nervously after Crymes as he quitted the Stand, though from not exactly the same motives. Mrs. Charrington really was more earnest than she was wont to be in her flirtations, and did know that bad falls occurred in steeple-chasing, as when out-paced horses are called upon to jump must be the case, however clever they may be, while Miss Aysgarth was much perturbed at the Major's last speech. She knew, as women always do know, that devoted though he might be to Mrs. Charrington, he was also an admirer of herself, but she had never pictured his admiration as taking practical form before, and yet, if he did not cherish some hope of avowing it, what could his last words mean? Let them mean what they might, one thing was conclusive, they contained a menace to Cis as regarded the forthcoming race, and she was so anxious that he should be hailed the winner, not only because of the heavy bets he had upon it, but because of some small superstitions of her own that had come to associate it with her marriage very much in the manner Horace Crymes had darkly hinted.

The crowd began now to throng the rails of the 'run in' to see the horses canter before going down to the starting-post, which laid a little to the left of the Stand, and the first to make its appearance was The Mumper; plain and common-looking he was pronounced by the lookers-on, and the north country race-goers know a horse when they see one, but for all that he was pronounced a nice goer when Cis Calvert, after the preliminary march past, brought him back again at a smart canter. Herodia, Red Lancer, and Gil Blas followed. Nice looking hunters, said the talent, but they don't steal over the ground like that old black, and lastly came Crymes upon The Cid. The Major brought his horse down again at a good rattling gallop, and a slight murmur of applause greeted the handsome grey as he swept by with his long, easy stride.

"Not the sort to be prejudiced against, Charrington," said Julian Harperley, "not yet quite the man, from the way we've seen him go."

"I don't believe in The Cid," remarked

the other grimly. "Mark me, Calvert will make a mess of him to-day."

The horses walk quietly down to the starting-post, gather together for a few minutes in a group, then the flag falls, and they are away.

"The Mumper leads!" exclaims one of those intelligent race-goers who can never by any accident get the colours into his head.

"Nothing of the sort," retorted Mr. Charrington sharply; "can't you see that's the second colour—black, red sleeves, and *black* cap; that's Red Lancer, and, by Jove! he's leading them a cracker. Herodia second, in green, and Gil Blas, in the pink and black cap close up, The Mumper's lying fourth (you may know him by the *red* cap), and The Cid's waiting on him."

Harry Harperley meanwhile was fulfilling his mission, which was to make running for Cis Calvert. Strangford on Herodia kept close with him for the best of all possible reasons; he knew his mare could stay for a week, but she was not fast, and her sole chance of winning was to lie in front all the way, and trust to her opponents cutting their throats. If he once let them get away from her he knew she had not speed enough ever to catch them again. As for young Radcliffe, as he frankly said, he meant having 'a ride,' he didn't affect much jockeyship, and prudently held, under these circumstances, he had best keep with the leaders as long as he could, and quietly succumb when he found that no longer possible. He had very slight hope of winning, and had indeed backed The Cid for a pony, though he would have willingly jobbed the last ounce out of his horse to win the Cup.

Red Lancer was a fine fencer, and Harry Harperley streamed away with the lead, jealously attended by Herodia and Gil Blas, while as for the two leading characters in the drama they laid off, watching one another like two practised duellists when first confronted. No change occurred in the order of running till nigh half the course was compassed, by which time the three in front held such a commanding lead, that a cry rose from the Stand, "They'll never catch them. By heavens, the two favourites are out of it!"

The very next fence made a change in the aspect of things, for slipping up at the take off, Gil Blas tumbled ignominiously into the next field, leaving his rider to taste earth and see stars, and enjoy all the luxuries of a regular crumpler. But no sooner had he cleared the jump than it appeared to Cis Calvert it was getting high time to get on terms with his leaders, and gradually he commenced lessening the gap between them, while the dangerous Cid hung tenaciously at his quarters. Still Red Lancer raced away with the command, till as they rounded the flag for home Harry Harperley felt that his bolt was shot, and without a struggle yielded the lead to Strangford. Cool as ever, the latter steadied his mare, and with a quaint chuckle remarked to himself, "Two of them cooked! but oh, dear, I suppose I shall have the swells alongside directly full of running, and we can't go much faster, can we, old woman?"

Herodia was doing her best, and her rider knew it. Scant hope of his winning the cup, if he were collared, and just as he arrived at this conclusion he became conscious of The Mumper creeping up on his whip hand. One glance at the black told him he was out of it, for Calvert's horse was striding along, full of running, and as fresh apparently as when he started. Another second and the grey appeared on the off side, also going strong and well.

"A race between you, gentlemen!" cried Strangford, as they passed him, "but I'll follow on just to see the finish."

Cis had now taken the lead, and was making the pace hot. For the first time in the race the Major's face darkened, and there was a slight nervous twitch of his upper lip. They were fairly in the straight run in, and niggling a little at his horse, and kneeing him a bit besides, Crymes ran up to take a feeler. He set his teeth grimly as the fact dawned upon him that the old black had the heels of him, and his sole chance laid in giving him a fall. There were but three fences now over which to do it, and Crymes deliberately drove The Cid at the next stake and binder with a view to putting his adversary down by rushing him at his fence. But Cis, lying a good length and a half ahead, and finding his horse going strong and well, had made up his mind to come straight away, and stand no more nonsense. He shook up The Mumper, and, to the Major's surprise, went right away from him. Putting him down was out of the question, for the black, when it came to racing, was unmistakably the quicker horse of the two, and catch him

Crymes could not. He rode the race out steadily and judgmatically, as usual, on the off chance, but Cis Calvert passed the winning-post a good half-dozen lengths in front of him, and the Major was too good a sportsman to cut up a beaten horse in hopeless pursuit.

"Chucked away! chucked away!" exclaimed Mr. Boggs, as he witnessed the finish of the race. "Why the old black beggar's a stone better than I thought him."

"Yes," rejoined Mr. Blundell, ruefully, "it is as you say, 'chucked away.' Our good thing is about as handsomely spilt as any milk I ever saw handed about. I did think you knew The Mumper's form, at all events."

"You think!" said Boggs, "don't you overheat those precious brains of yours by thinking. There's your fifty in Bank of England notes; and now off with you like a sky-rocket, and hand that note to your master at once. Tell him it's immediate, and to read it before he weighs in. Off with you, quick, if you ever expect to see the other fifty."

That fifty pounds in his hand, and the ascendancy Isham had acquired over him, sufficed to send Blundell best pace in pursuit of his master.

Horace Crymes, very sore at heart, was walking his horse slowly back to the saddling enclosure, when Blundell met him, and handed him the note with which he had been entrusted. The Major had lost a biggish stake on the race, and money was money to him just now, but it was not that, he was far too practised a turfite to succumb under a reverse. No prouder man ever stepped than Crymes, and the result of the race had wounded him sorely on that point. Where was his bitter boast to Miss Aysgarth now? How shall he ever bear Charrington's cackle over the proverbial softness of grey horses? He had gone down in front of the ladies' gallery, and his character for omniscience in everything sporting would no longer be a recognized fact in the regiment.

He crushed the note mechanically in his hand as Blundell led The Cid into the paddock, slipped lightly off his horse, ungirthed the saddle, and, throwing it over his arm, walked mechanically towards the weighing-room.

"The note, sir, the note!" whispered Blundell, eagerly. "I don't know what's in it, but I was bid tell you to read it before you got into the scales."

Crymes looked at him for a minute, and then, entering the weighing-room, gazed sullenly at his successful adversary, who, saddle in lap, was going through the crucial test of Turf victory. He dropped his eyes, and, opening the paper in his hand, glanced over it.

A triumphant smile swept across his dark face as he did so, and no sooner had Calvert vacated the scales than Crymes seated himself lightly in his place. Hardly had the clerk pronounced 'all right' than the Major, rising to his feet, exclaimed, "Is there a steward present?"

"Of course, Crymes. What is it?" replied Colonel Copplestone.

"A somewhat unpleasant business, sir, I am afraid, but I have no alternative. If it was my own money only it might go to the devil, but I have a large following who have staked their money on The Cid, and that leaves me nothing to do but to enter a formal objection against The Mumper as being a well-known steeple-chaser, and as such utterly unqualified to run for a regimental race. Captain Calvert's black horse, The Mumper, is better known as the Black Doctor, and has hit the ring hard many times down Warwick and Worcester way."

"Good God, Crymes! are you sure you have warrant for what you say?"

"It's not likely, Colonel, I should make

such a charge unless I deemed I had conclusive evidence."

And in the doorway stood two men, paralyzed by these terrible words, Cis Calvert and Julian Harperley, who had come to congratulate him on his success.

CHAPTER XI.

THE OBJECTION.

For a few seconds Cis stood spell-bound by the charge brought against him; then he stepped rapidly back into the weighing-room, and, in a voice tremulous with passion, exclaimed—

"Whether this is the case or not, do you mean to insinuate, Major Crymes, that I have wittingly run this horse as The Mumper, being aware all the time that he was a well-known steeple-chaser?"

"I should hope not," rejoined Crymes coldly, "though, considering the manner in which you have backed him, I am afraid the world will perhaps put an ugly construction on your mistake. No, don't interrupt me for one moment, Calvert. I knew nothing about this till the race was run, or I should have told you what I had heard. The information reached me on my way here just now. I have my backers both in the regiment and elsewhere; in their interests I am bound to enter this protest."

"But, good God!" cried Cis, "whether this story is true or no, you can surely not believe that I knew anything about the horse's private history? You know how I bought him."

"I must decline any discussion of the subject, and allow me to point out, have made no sort of accusation against you. This is all matter for the stewards, not for you or me."

"Excuse me!" cried Cis hotly, "you know perfectly well that if you accuse me of entering a well-known steeple-chaser in another name, and my brother officers believe that charge, I am a ruined man."

"As I have already remarked," returned Crymes, with exasperating coolness, "I make no accusation of any kind."

"Liar!" cried Cis furiously; "what else is your objection? what else can it mean?"

For a second a savage scowl darkened the Major's face, and he took a quick step or two towards his opponent, then mastering himself with a mighty effort he turned and said in low-measured tones—"Colonel Copplestone, I put myself in your hands both as a steward and my commanding officer." Simultaneously Julian Harperley secured Cis by the arm, and said, "For heaven's sake, my good fellow, restrain yourself!"

"Captain Calvert, you will return at once to barracks, and consider yourself under arrest," exclaimed the Colonel. "Such language you well know can be tolerated to no brother officer, more especially to one your senior in rank. Your objection, Major Crymes, will of course be due subject of inquiry for myself and brother stewards at once, and you will of course produce such evidence as you consider necessary to substantiate such a very serious charge."

Foaming with passion, it was perhaps questionable whether Cis would have yielded to Julian Harperley's remonstrance, but the habit of discipline is strong, and the curt, pithy order of his Colonel curbed him at once, and touching his cap to the chief he turned to obey his command.

Outside the weighing-room he was met by Harry Harperley and other friends, who had come to congratulate him on his success, but already the ominous whisper of an objection had got about, and instead of felicitations they inquired anxiously what was the matter?

"Trouble's the matter, Harry," said poor Cis, quickly, "trouble more than I can quite understand as yet. I'm in an awful mess, boy. Steal or borrow me a hack, and bring it up here at once. I've to ride back to barracks at once. I'm in arrest."

He had all the audacity natural to the cornet of a crack regiment, but 'arrest' to his youthful mind, having reference to an officer, presented a disturbed vision of pains, penalties, and disgrace beyond apprehension. Not only was he very fond of Cis himself, but he knew instinctively that this would bring sore sorrow upon his sister besides, and he loved her very dearly. If he did not know of her tacit engagement, he, at all events, was quite awake to Cis being what he called 'heavy spoons' on Annie, and the arrangement met with this young gentleman's unqualified approval. It was with a sad heart he hurried off to find his own horse, and bring it up for his captain to ride home on.

"Mr. Harperley," exclaimed Cis, "I trust you don't believe this infamous accusation!"

"Bearing in mind that you know nothing

about the horse," rejoined the banker, "I am afraid that Major Crymes is perhaps better informed. Remember, I say distinctly that I believe you know nothing about the horse, but you must forgive me adding that, though I can make every allowance for your unfortunate loss of temper, I am afraid it has dreadfully complicated the business. At present, if you will allow me to be your adviser, I think there is nothing for you but to do what you propose; ride quietly home, and await the upshot of events."

"If he didn't say I was a downright leg, he insinuated it," retorted Cis angrily.

"It was a cruel charge to have brought against one, and that your blood should boil over far from unnatural, but as a looker on, Calvert, I must testify that Major Crymes brought his objection forward without throwing the slightest imputation upon yourself. He, to divest it of sporting phraseology, denounced a fraud, but he certainly did not denounce *you* in connection with it."

"Perhaps not in words, but he did in manner," rejoined Cis sullenly.

"No, I can hardly bear you out in that. Remember, you were naturally excited, and imagined innuendos that were never intended. Pray don't think I am either deserting you, much less taking part against you, but if Crymes proves his case it is bound to prove an unpleasant business. No one will be more glad to see you triumphantly through it than I shall."

"And you will tell Annie you still believe in me," said Cis in a low voice, as Harry reappeared, followed by his groom leading his horse.

"If Crymes proves his assertion," rejoined Julian Harperley, "that is nothing. As I said just now, he has never alleged that you were cognizant of the imposture."

"Good-bye," rejoined Cis, as he swung himself into the saddle; then leaning over to young Harperley he said, "Come and tell me, Harry, what they decide about the objection. I can only solemnly declare that if it is so, Crymes knows a great deal more about the horse than I do."

All who have had anything to do with racing know what a stir and confusion an objection creates. The Major's protest was quite in accordance with the usual ordering of such things; considerable consternation on the part of not only the backers of The Mumper, but also on that of Mr. Beilton and some of the leading ring men, who had been somehow inspired to lay more than was good for them against The Cid. In the Stand, amongst the ladies, curiosity was on tiptoe to know the true state of the case, but none of the actors in the drama reappeared.

"Where was Major Crymes?" asked Mrs. Charrington. "Where was Captain Calvert? Mr. Harperley, &c.? what was the objection? who objected? who then had won?" Such were the questions bandied about, and for the answering of which, no reliable male creature could be found available. At last came intelligence that The Mumper was not The Mumper, but alleged to be something else; what, rumour was not so clear about. He was a steeplechaser of distinction, he had won races here, there, everywhere; he had won the Liverpool, he had won it twice, thrice; the absurdity of describing such an animal as a hunter! Could this have been an accident? Somebody must have known. Somebody must have meant winning money over it? Who? and then somehow a whisper got about that Captain Calvert had backed his horse for a big stake. First it was told that there had been a violent scene in the weighing-room between the Major and Cis Calvert, and that the latter had left the course in high dudgeon; and finally it was darkly hinted that Captain Calvert had left the course in obedience ot the strongly-expressed recommendation of the stewards, who had pronounced him guilty of practice somewhat sharper than could be tolerated amongst gentlemen in Yorkshire.

Poor Annie Aysgarth sat feeling utterly miserable whilst all these *canards* surged around her; not a quarter of an hour ago, and, with triumphant smile on lip and brow, she was eagerly waiting to greet her lover as he returned the recognized hero of the day; and now why did he not come to her? How dare these women even hint such foul shame concerning him? Where was her father? Where was Harry? The girl had plenty of pluck, and believed thoroughly in Cis. She would laugh to scorn the suggestion that he could be guilty of aught dishonourable. She would have pledged her life upon his truth and loyalty in any matter, and it was exceeding bitter to her to listen to all these evil whispers concerning him, and not to be able to break a lance in his defence. More than once her indignation nearly overcame her better judgment, and prompted her to flash out and ask fiercely, "You know Captain Calvert most of you; what have you ever seen in him to induce you to think that he would do anything dishonourable? In common justice give the benefit the law allows, and hold him innocent till he is proved guilty." But then, unluckily, she was not openly affianced to this man, and so shrank, as was natural, from taking up the cudgels in his behalf.

Very right was Miss Aysgarth theoretically, but practically she would have done little good had she given her thoughts words. A man is held guiltless in the eye of the law till he is proved guilty, but in the eye of society! bah! we know it is exactly the reverse; he is held guilty till he proves his innocence. It is this at times makes hard the pleasant fictions of society's journals. In the days when The Mumper won the Cup these conservators of the public morals did not exist; it was possible to commit card-sharping at Nice, and not have it advertised the same week in London; divers peccadilloes might be then freely indulged in, and the world none the wiser, but in these times, good lack! we must look well to our morals, and—and—well, let us hope at least they've improved.

At last Mr. Harperley makes his appearance in search of his daughter, and has to run a very gauntlet of interrogatories, to which he responds, that he believes the stewards have not yet given their decision, but that he understands The Mumper will be probably disqualified, having won a public steeple-chase or two before he came into Captain Calvert's hands, though quite unknown to that gentleman.

"Come along, Annie," he whispers, "the carriage is at the back of the Stand, and I don't think the Farmers' Race worth our waiting for under the circumstances. I will tell you what has happened, as far as I know, presently, but it is a very unpleasant affair, and has taken all the fun out of the meeting. From Colonel Copplestone down to Harry the —th Lancers are looking glum as undertakers over the result. Winners or losers, it seems to make little difference. Come, child, at once, I want to get away without further questioning."

The girl takes her father's arm, and as they make their way out she catches glances, shrugs, and half-smothered whispers, and knows that they are talking about her, as if it were possible to keep such secrets as that of her tacit engagement with Cis; and once more the indignant blood mantles in her face, for she feels that they are pitying her on account of her lover, and to a proud young woman such as Annie Aysgarth, who gloried and believed implicitly in her sweetheart, could anything be more humiliating? As they drove back to The Firs, Julian Harperley told his daughter as much as he had been able to gather of the affair, but as the banker had not been present at the conference of the stewards, he was not much wiser concerning the racing objection than he had been in the first instance, but he had seen what may be termed the military embroglio, and did not hesitate to tell Annie that he feared Cis, by loss of temper, had very much further complicated an already sufficiently awkward business.

The girl was silent for a second, then she said, in clear resonant tones, "Neither you nor I, papa, could imagine Cis doing anything dishonourable, but I am grieved about this quarrel with Major Crymes. It is likely to create prejudice against him."

She would not have realized what such breach of military etiquette as Cis had committed really involved, even if her father had told her, but the banker had described the scene in the weighing-room as "high words passed between Crymes and Calvert," without specifying that one significant monosyllable which from time immemorial it has been held that no gentleman can pass over.

But it speedily became apparent that all life was crushed out of the company assembled in the Stand. That vague feeling of something having gone wrong, which suffices to so rapidly break up any party of pleasure, was evidently abroad. Neither Major Crymes nor young Harperley reappeared, and, though Colonel Copplestone and some of the officers did their best to keep things going, yet there was a general stampede. It was of course known that The Mumper had been disqualified for having, unknown to his owner, won a public steeple-chase previously; but society, as it made its way home from Crockley Hill, came to the conclusion that there was more to tell than had leaked out as yet.

Harry Harperley, as one of the gentlemen riding in the race, had of course no trouble in making his way into the weighing-room, where the stewards, consisting of two officers of the Lancers and three well-known members of the Hunt, were sitting in judgment. Crymes briefly stated his case, pointed out that this knowledge had only come to him after the race was run, and that, in justice to his numerous backers, he had no alternative but to bring it before the stewards.

The evidence was overwhelming, there could be no doubt that The Mumper and the Black Doctor were one and the same horse, and that under the latter name he had a few years back been a steeple-chase horse of no little celebrity. The Mumper was accordingly disqualified, and the race awarded to The Cid.

Harry Harperley had only stayed to hear the decision. No sooner was it pronounced than he jumped into Radcliffe's 'whitechapel,' which was waiting for him at the back of the Stand. That young gentleman was his sworn ally, and, like himself, a firm believer in Cis Calvert, and the pair were very seriously concerned about the aspect of things. The insult Cis had passed upon Crymes had certainly not been before all the world, as the saying goes, but still there had been some half-dozen people present, and something of the truth had already oozed out. When six people conspire, one usually acquaints those whom it is most desirable to keep in ignorance with all particulars; though in Ireland I am told six conspirators produce as a rule seven informers, and judging from the *cacoethes loquendi* displayed by Irish members of Parliament, it is easy to imagine so; therefore it was not to be much wondered at that some account of the quarrel between the two men was about.

"I shall be at mess, Radcliffe," said Harry, as the trap pulled up in front of the officers' quarters, "if it is only to hear what our fellows think of all this business. In the mean time I must run up and tell Calvert what the stewards' decision was."

Radcliffe nodded. "It's rough on him, but this row with Crymes is the trouble. I don't think any one in the regiment would believe Cis was wittingly committing a fraud, and any horse that has ever won public money is, we know, not qualified to run for the Cup."

Calvert was sitting, looking somewhat moodily into the fire, when the cornet entered, but roused himself immediately, and exclaimed, "Now, Harry, let's hear all about it. I fancy Crymes knows a deal more about The Mumper than I do."

"The Major first made his objection, as you may suppose, laying particular stress upon the point that he knew nothing of The Mumper's history till after the race. Then that Dick Hunsley Mappin told us of appeared, there were plenty there who knew him, and stated he had bought the horse in the spring of last year in Warwickshire; that he knew him as the Black Doctor, and his performances were on record in the 'Calendar'; he had bought him merely to hunt, and changed his name, as he didn't want to be chaffed about riding a steeplechaser. He told of whom he had bought him, and the groom who had fetched the horse from Warwickshire was there to testify to the fact; but further than that he had fetched the horse from there at the time stated, his evidence was of little consequence, as he did not know the horse's name. Hunsley next produced a letter, dated a few days back, in which William Gurwood stated, in answer to a letter he had received on the question, that he had sold the Black Doctor, by Dicebox out of Ebony, to Richard Hunsley on the 20th of April, '51, for value received."

"And they seemed to think there was no doubt about this story?" asked Cis.

"No; they sent for Mappin, who gave the same account of how The Mumper came into his possession that he had already given to you. The story sounded only too true, and as that precious rascal, Dick Hunsley, said, 'If I'm not telling the truth, gentlemen, it's mighty easy to send into Warwickshire and see Gurwood; you've got his address."

"Yes, it can scarcely be a vamped-up story, but it is hard lines the terrible scrape it has got me into."

"Well, now there comes a point which I can't help thinking was in your favour. You don't for one moment suppose, Cis, that any of us doubt your good faith in the business," interposed the boy quickly, "but there are some don't know you as we do."

"You're loyal, very loyal, to your captain, Harry," replied Calvert with a faint smile.

"As if we won't all stand by you; but what I was going to say was this:—Charrington, a steward, as you know, although he declined to act on this occasion, having, as he said, bets on the race, was present; suddenly he scribbled a few lines on a leaf of his betting-book, and passing it to the chief, said, 'I think, Colonel Copplestone, you would find it useful to ask this question.' The chief showed it to the other officials, and then with their assent inquired:

"'Why, Mr. Hunsley, knowing all this, did you not interfere earlier?'

"'It was no business of mine,' was the sulky response.

"'But there has been plenty of betting in York about this race; there was a good deal, for instance, I understand, at Harker's last night. You must have known all the time that The Mumper had no right to start. Why did you not let Captain Calvert or some of us know the state of the case?'

"For a second Dick Hunsley looked puzzled, then a sullen scowl darkened his face. 'Well, if you will have the truth, gentlemen, you shall. Why didn't I? Because it suited my book not to do so. I had a score to settle, and money to get by it, and I've been racing too long not to collar coin when I can, and cry quits with those who've put me in the hole. The man who sold me up was backing The Mumper, and I—well, I backed the Cid.'

"'Thank you, Mr. Hunsley, I don't think we need trouble you further,' said the chief, and that's how the case stands, Cis."

"I should hope Hunsley's evidence is sufficient to exonerate me from all imputation of knowing The Mumper's previous history," replied Calvert, "but I am in a big scrape besides that. I am in arrest, as you know, and can hardly guess how that matter will finish; then I've had a baddish race of it besides. I only hope you hadn't much on The Mumper."

"No, I took that two hundred to fifteen from Strangford, and had a tenner on my mount, that's all. I've lost a pony, and that matters little, but I'm terribly grieved about you."

"Pooh!" rejoined Cis, "I shall pull through. Give my love to your sister, tell her what you have told me, and tell her—you can, Harry, can't you?—that you don't believe I am capable of such a piece of rascality as winning the Cup by a shameful fraud. That I rode and won in all innocence that my horse was anything but the hunter I bought him as."

"I don't think any one of your friends will ever suppose anything else," cried Harry, with a slight gulp in his throat. He was cruelly hurt at the foul imputations he had already heard whispered against his captain, and had not learnt to avoid display of his best feelings as we do mostly later on in life. "Now I must run away and dress for mess," and Cis and his cornet exchanged one of those hand grips into which Englishmen condense a flood of sentimental language.

But when Harry Harperley had left the room, Cis reverted to that very much grimmer view of the situation he had been musing over before the youngster had entered. He knew that his quarrel with Crymes might probably become a serious thing for him, so serious, indeed, as to necessitate his retirement from the service; then he had lost, for him, a very heavy sum of money, and unluckily the bulk of it to Crymes, all of which had to be forthcoming in two or three days. Two circumstances these to make the victim thereof regard the last twelve hours as an ill-spent day. How marvellously penitent and filled with good intentions I have seen men on the day after the Derby; but to what extent rancorous tongues, combined with unfortunate appearances, can mar a man's life Cis has yet to learn. A very imperfect idea as to what constitutes hard lines as yet seething in his brain.

END OF VOL. I.

www.ingramcontent.com/pod-product-compliance
Lightning Source LLC
Chambersburg PA
CBHW020513270326
41926CB00008B/856